How to Win at CRM

How to Win at CRM
Strategy, Implementation, Management

Seth J. Kinnett

CRC Press
Taylor & Francis Group
Boca Raton London New York

CRC Press is an imprint of the
Taylor & Francis Group, an **informa** business

AN AUERBACH BOOK

CRC Press
Taylor & Francis Group
6000 Broken Sound Parkway NW, Suite 300
Boca Raton, FL 33487-2742

Printed on acid-free paper

International Standard Book Number-13 978-1-4987-1470-9 (Hardback)

Library of Congress Cataloging-in-Publication Data

Names: Kinnett, Seth, author.
Title: How to win at CRM : strategy, implementation, management / Seth Kinnett.
Description: Boca Raton, FL : CRC Press, 2017.
Identifiers: LCCN 2017011251 | ISBN 9781498714709 (hardback)
Subjects: LCSH: Customer relations--Data processing. | Customer relations--Marketing.
Classification: LCC HF5415.5 .G539 2017 | DDC 658.8/12--dc23
LC record available at https://lccn.loc.gov/2017011251

Visit the Taylor & Francis Web site at
http://www.taylorandfrancis.com

and the CRC Press Web site at
http://www.crcpress.com

Disclaimer: The views and opinions are the author's own and do not represent the views or opinions of the author's employers or colleagues, past or present.

Dedication

For Greg Schwipps & Dave Berque
Teachers, Mentors, Friends

Contents

Preface

The choice to write about customer relationship management (CRM) was in some ways an obvious one, given that it had been my professional focus for over a decade. When I was assigned to my first CRM project many years ago, I had no idea that I would begin a specialization in what has become one of the most influential concepts and pieces of software in corporate enterprise. Many organizations have developed a soft spot for CRM. Yet the more they attempt to assuage it, enhance it, extend it, the more they push users away. CRM success continues to elude us.

CRM has become synonymous with an enterprise technology platform. Many have written of the mistakes in this paradigm. They note that the idea of CRM is a cultural orientation and influences all aspects of running a successful business. Much has also been written about the importance of mastering business processes before attempting to automate them. Sometimes, however, it seems as if these recommendations suggest that the particulars of the technology product chosen to execute upon the organization's streamlined business processes and cultural commitment to CRM are ignored. But there are specific decisions made daily in the trenches of the technical implementation of CRM which are making notable contributions to an organization's ability to achieve success with its CRM initiatives. The technology matters, and it matters a lot.

The purpose of this text is to provide clarity and guidance on effective strategy, implementation, and management of CRM. We will explore both the conceptual and cultural contexts of CRM initiatives along with the particulars of CRM system implementation and management. In order to provide this clarity, we have surveyed the existing academic publications surrounding CRM, sales force automation, and related topics within Information Systems literature. This research has been supplemented by insights from CRM experts to provide a robust picture of the CRM landscape and how to improve it no matter what role you play within your organization. Whether you are an IT professional, salesperson, senior executive, sales manager, marketing manager, or otherwise want to achieve CRM success, this book is for you.

Throughout each stage of this book, we will examine functional, technical, and psychological considerations, understanding that each of these areas must be mastered to achieve CRM success. This text does not intend to endorse, disparage, or otherwise provide commentary on any existing CRM product. All scenarios explored herein are original and not leveraged from actual events, and they reference no actual firms or individuals. The views in this book are mine and are not reflective of the views of any of my employers or colleagues, past or present.

Despite all efforts to explore in depth all facets of CRM, the landscape is always changing. To stay on top of the latest trends, listen and subscribe to podcasts, and to learn more about how to find assistance in translating the topics we discuss in this book into big wins for your firm, please visit the book's companion website: www. howtowinatcrm.com.

Having now spent over 12 years in both the consulting and corporate sides of CRM, I trust that the perspectives and insights throughout the book will be relevant and helpful to you. Ultimately, I hope this information will not only make your firm successful, but also afford you a better professional quality of life.

Best of luck,
Seth J. Kinnett

Acknowledgments

This book would not have been possible without the support of my many excellent teachers, professors, friends, and family. Long ago I promised my grandmother, Lettie Bellinger, that I would write a book, and here it is. I'm grateful to her and all of the Bellingers and Kinnetts for their support over the years. My special thanks to my parents, Joe and Linda, who I owe so much.

I would like to thank the Computer Science and English faculties at DePauw University, especially Dave Berque, Greg Schwipps, Chris White, Beth Benedix, Tom Chiarella, and Rick Hillis. My DePauw experience was life-changing, and I could easily write paragraphs about the impact that each of these excellent professors had on my scholarship and life overall.

Daren Tedeschi—back in Oxford in 2004, you told me the secret to winning—the proverbial Wicket Key to unlock success. Thank you. Those days at Oxford truly were life-changing, the foundation of so much. Would that we could be back there tomorrow. Thank you to my indispensable Oxford tutor, Kevin K. Shortsleeve, who set the highest bar for my writing and never gave up on making sure I cleared it.

Gene Brewer—you have been a superior mentor. You showed me it really is worth it to press on through the relentless challenges to achieve victory. Those thoughts carried me through many a rough day when it seemed like things would never come together.

Thanks to some of my biggest supporters: Bastion Crider, Ben Crider, Laurence Jankelow, Kate Ireland, Erica Sanchez, Richard Leung, Brendan Hula, Paras Baxi, Ankeet Patel, Brian Nannini, Renée Briglio, Jamie Briglio, Sean Cisney, Chad Hossfield, Eric Ossipow, Bonnie Goins, Marissa McCaw, and Sam Kinnett. And in so many countless ways which I doubt I could ever fully articulate, my eternal gratitude to Drs. Robert Wyllie, David Magnuson, Douglas Rogers, Emre Gorgun, Laura Yun, Mike McGee, and Bo Shen.

We would not have been able to win at CRM without the generosity of those who contributed their time and expertise. Thanks to Tim Kippley and Brad Schneider of Rightpoint Consulting for their strong contributions and to Clayton Wolff for all of his help. And of course, it's impossible to spell CRM without Jake Schomp. I've learned so much from him and I'm grateful for it. To all of you collectively: there is no doubt that we are smarter and better as a result of your insights.

My extra special thanks to Chanté Brown, Michael Howard, Haley Cannon, and all of the staff of the Dollop Coffee & Tea Company, Buena Park, Chicago, for their interest, encouragement, and kindness.

Finally, thanks to the editorial team—Richard Tressider, Ananth Ganesan—and all the folks at CRC Press for their hard work bringing this to market. Thank you especially to my publisher, Rich O'Hanley, for his unwavering support of this project.

About the Author

Seth J. Kinnett has over 12 years of professional CRM experience in both consulting and industry. He holds a BA in Computer Science and English Writing from DePauw University and an MS in Information Technology & Management from Illinois Institute of Technology. He lives in Chicago.

PART I
STRATEGY

1
THERE'S SOMETHING ABOUT CRM

Customer relationship management (CRM) has exploded in popularity over the past two decades. The potential value of CRM has been recognized throughout virtually all industry verticals, and CRM initiatives have been embraced by companies of all market capitalizations. Everyone wants to be a star player in the CRM game. When implemented correctly, CRM can satisfy a number of critical objectives, including lowering the cost of customer acquisition, increasing customer retention and satisfaction, building customer loyalty, segmenting customers for targeted marketing initiatives, and identifying cross-selling opportunities—all while reducing operational costs and increasing operational efficiency.

The noted research firm, Gartner, as of the writing of this book, anticipates that CRM will become a 36-billion-dollar market by 2017. From 2012 to 2017, CRM has shown a compounded annual growth rate of 15.1%, leading all categories of enterprise software in projected growth, and is on track to eclipse enterprise resource planning (ERP) systems in global market size in 2017. However, despite all of its promises and relentless market expansion, CRM has rapidly fallen out of many firms' good graces as these firms struggle with myriad problems, including lack of clear CRM strategy, misalignment of business goals to the technical execution of these goals, and keeping CRM systems running, current, and usable. As a result of the vast potential surrounding CRM, folks working in the CRM space are under significant pressure and scrutiny—perhaps at a level unparalleled by those working in other areas of the enterprise. This is the result of several factors—most notably that CRM has such a direct link to the customer, to revenue, to success.

When analyzing CRM failures, a large portion of both academic literature and professional publications admonish firms for neglecting to consider the business process, not being customer centric, or placing too much faith in the technology. Instead of taking a magnifying glass to the specific implementations of CRM technology, many firms embark on soul-searching strategy quests, emerging with admissions that they may just not focus enough on customers—as if they had not previously considered that customers were important to running a business. The reality is that achieving CRM success is a result of understanding and taking action to improve upon certain functional, psychological, and technical realities. Our lens—perhaps more than any existing book on CRM—will examine just how important technology and organizational psychological phenomena precipitate CRM failure just as often as poor process understanding or implementation.

To begin with, to underscore how—in CRM especially—the quality of technology is so important, we need look no further than a study that examined the impact of three key enterprise systems on profitability and stock price. The systems studied were ERP systems, supply chain management (SCM) systems, and—our favorite—CRM systems. The study made no differentiation between well-designed and adopted CRM systems versus poor implementations, and the authors concluded that "investments in CRM systems had little effect on the stock returns of investing firms."[1] They further noted that "investments in CRM systems seem to have had little impact on profitability."[1] In the same study, SCM systems—also evaluated straight-up, not considering adoption, usability, or software quality—almost universally contributed to higher profits and stock prices for the surveyed firms. The very presence of a SCM system yielded benefits. Is it because all SCM systems are implemented flawlessly? Or is there something about CRM that is different?

While studying the ins and outs of supply chain software is not within the scope of this book, we can see that there is something going on here and that the effective implementation of CRM—while drawing parallels from other pieces of enterprise software—is unique. We will examine the distinctions at length, but we can briefly note two key differences: audience and complexity. First, salespeople are notoriously resistant to embrace technology, and second, CRM relies more on what might be called "soft data" than other systems. Events in the market may cause CRM systems to be required to be adapted more often than other enterprise systems, which leads to a need for agility that some CRM implementations are not prepared to address. Before going much further down the CRM rabbit hole, let us begin by examining the semantics of CRM so that we have a clear picture of exactly what it is we are exploring.

What Is CRM?

CRM is the acronym for customer relationship management, and colloquially, it can refer to a concept or a specific type of technology system. Often when people say CRM, what they are really talking about are *CRM applications*, which are defined in a study by Liu, Liu, and Xu in 2013 as "enterprise information systems that digitize business processes at the customer-facing end of the value chain, including marketing, sales and post-sales support."[2] We might also refer to CRM applications as CRM technology, as does another study that aims to clarify CRM applications as a *component* of CRM, specifically defining CRM technology as "the information technology that is deployed for the specific purpose of managing customer relationships."[3] Referring to CRM when we *mean* CRM applications—that is, conflating concept with mechanism—is considered by some to be one of the core drivers of CRM failure. The idea here is that people view CRM too narrowly, seeing it only as a piece of technology rather than a broader strategy woven into the web of a firm's culture. If only people would understand that it is so much more than technology, some have reasoned, CRM would be successful.

CRM, the concept, is defined in many similar but distinct ways. Many of the varied definitions are really distinctions without differences. A study by Saxena and Khandelwal in 2011 succinctly and effectively defined CRM, the concept, as "the process of organizing business activities around customers."[4] It was in the 1990s that the focus of sales and marketing began to shift—we might say evolved— from transactional to relationship-based marketing. Transactional marketing was characterized by its focus around product, price, place, and promotion—sometimes known as the four Ps. The core difference between these two approaches is relationship marketing's focus on creating a picture of a customer and nurturing a relationship through the long haul. As salespeople have known for years, it is easier to retain an existing customer than to prospect a new one, and relationship orientation helps to facilitate retention. Fortunately, CRM also aids in prospecting and acquisition.

Tim Kippley, CRM Practice Lead at Chicago-based Rightpoint Consulting, stated that the broad and varying definitions of CRM were one of the biggest surprises he observed at firms throughout his 16 years of experience. He extended this point during a 2016 interview noting,

> People often perceive CRM—and good job to leading vendors for marketing their products so well—as a collection of tools and features. Philosophically, you can actually have a relationship without technology. The idea of having a relationship and leveraging that relationship to do business didn't dawn at the beginning of the computer. People were doing business long before that. Sometimes this reality gets lost. The technology is just enabling what we want to do naturally anyway. It's a supporting mechanism for that.[5]

Brad Schneider, cofounder of Rightpoint Consulting, recognizes that CRM tools have also evolved significantly since their inception. During a 2016 interview, he extended this point, explaining that "some of the tools we're using on a day-to-day basis have evolved to not just be what traditional CRM was, but—lots of times—we're looking at these as platforms for running people's businesses. It's been nice to see that evolution and see the different applications of CRM to see different viewpoints companies take when they use it."[5] We will explore the benefits and challenges of CRM as a platform solution in later chapters.

As we look to bring structure to our discussion of CRM, we can observe that some of the extant literature categorizes CRM as strategic CRM, operational CRM, analytical CRM, or interactive CRM. Some of the literature we will review in this book will use the term *sales force automation* (SFA), which is a technology tool with functionality including "managing customer information, appointments, handling time management and planning, generating daily/weekly reports, managing sales leads, creating quotes, and tracking customer communication."[6] SFA software was the precursor to what are now called CRM systems. The distinction is a small one, however, and what many firms have called a CRM system is actually a SFA system. SFA is a component of *operational CRM*, which is defined as software handling "sales force automation, campaign management, event-based marketing, opportunity management, product configuration and contact management solutions, *inter alia*."[7] This line is often blurred, however, with some studies considering SFA to be inclusive of functionality such as campaign management. In this text, we will consider all references to SFA to be analogous to operational CRM, which is the portion of CRM technology we explore most thoroughly.

We will also review *analytical CRM*, which "explores customer-related data to answer questions such as 'what should we offer this customer next?', 'what is this customer's propensity to churn?' or 'how can our customers be segmented for campaigning purposes?'"[7] *Interactive CRM*—that is, a CRM through which customers interface directly—will not be covered in this text. Placing our focus on operational CRM is not accidental. This component—the most critical component—of CRM seems to be lacking in glamour compared to analytical CRM. Dreaming up new data cubes is certainly more exciting than upgrading a piece of hardware. All data cubes are useless, however, if the operational CRM system—an important source feeding the analytics engine (which may also be receiving external data such as market metrics)—is poor. Investing in analytical CRM when operational CRM is a failure is like trying to paint a kitchen before you have dug the basement (Figure 1.1).

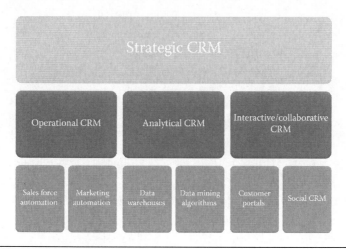

Figure 1.1 CRM categorization.

Why Pursue CRM Success?

Current research has shown myriad benefits resulting from the successful implementation of CRM, as well as the costs associated with failed CRM implementations. As one example to highlight the impact a poor CRM implementation may have on your company, consider the findings of a study conducted in 2006 by Ang and Buttle that highlighted the impact of a poor CRM system on a firm's human capital. The study found that CRM was "instrumental in causing sales people to leave the company after 6 months."[7]

Note that the impact is a direct hit to frontline salespeople, not an upstream frustration by sales management. In other words, the lack of, for example, analytics capabilities, while frustrating to management, is less likely to cause salesperson attrition than a slow, unreliable system that provides more headaches than benefits. While it may seem shocking that an enterprise software system could have such a large impact on as substantial a life decision as switching employers, the evidence shows us that it is indeed a real concern. We should also acknowledge that the deployments analyzed in this study also failed to contribute to increases in sales volumes or contracts. The authors do not note any decrease in sales volumes or contracts following CRM implementation, which contributes even further to our assertion that it is the human–technology component that fueled user attrition.

At the beginning of this chapter, we noted that CRM has become a hugely popular initiative for many organizations. The drivers for these initiatives encompass many different goals, and organizations engage in CRM initiatives for a variety of reasons. Tim Kippley, CRM Practice Lead at Rightpoint Consulting, Chicago, discussed some of those drivers for CRM during a 2016 interview:

> A lot of them [CRM implementation requests] will come surround some form around revenue. They've either acquired a company or they've changed their revenue model in some way. So they want to see what they can do to improve sales in that area. Also when there's internal turmoil. They may be unable to get an accurate view of things. Everybody has their own version of the truth and [these organizations] want to get to one consolidated version of the truth. Another one is

pipeline issues—less now but more so early on. They say "I can't forecast my business. I need to be able to run my business effectively." That's fundamental.[5]

Kippley also noted that particularly professional services firms realize that they are not selling widgets. They know that understanding what relationships exist and the strength of those relationships leads to the best opportunities to win business. Kippley's observations speak largely of the broad goals of CRM as a strategy—revenue generation, forecasting, and getting to a single version of the truth. Firms that have had CRM for a long time may benefit from reviewing some of those core fundamentals as sometimes firms are embarking on CRM for far more tactical reasons than just to keep their organizations running. A CRM expert who specializes in large enterprise implementations for Fortune 500 companies explains the organizational context of firms embarking on these types of CRM initiatives, noting,

> Most times, firms are trying to replace legacy systems which are expensive to maintain, lagging in innovation, can't keep pace with the business. Typically the business has voiced enough concern and complained enough to drive the technology team to be forced to make a decision. Are we going to continue to support an old system that's outdated and not improving or are we going to move to a platform that's going to make us flexible and responsive and even lead in marketplace conditions? Large companies understand if they're not advancing their technology platforms, their competition is going to leave them in the dust. They know they have to move with the market or get left behind.[7]

These sentiments are largely based on technology. This reveals both that some organizations may be viewing CRM as only a system and neglecting the process component, as much of the research implores us to do, and also that poor technical implementations are a real, tangible concern for organizations to the point where they have prioritized spending on correcting them. CRM has reached a certain level of market maturity, and both the consultants interviewed for this book confirmed that highlighting a large quantity of their business comes in the reimplementation space, often due to poor adoption. The anonymous consultant provided additional insights:

> Most companies have CRM, but there are absolutely divisions within a company. These large enterprise global corporations that are not using CRM whatsoever. It's often many business units, teams, within the organization [who have not adopted CRM]. Entire departments within world class companies completely operating outside of the CRM environment. They're operating with a Word document on an Excel sheet across a team of ten people and they're emailing it around and these are world class companies and they have departments that are not driven to use technology to its fullest they're not aware of the benefits of having a CRM available to all team members.[8]

Brad Schneider of Rightpoint Consulting confirmed that "a lot of the work we see is in the reimplementation world. We're implementing it for companies which have tried it once, twice, three times before but they've found users aren't using the system because they don't understand the value it's adding to their business."[5] This lack of understanding of CRM's value speaks to the importance of organizations selling CRM to the business. From a theoretical perspective, firms have the opportunity to harness the Hawthorne effect, which states that "employees are more productive based on their belief that changes made to the environment will increase productivity."[9] It could be useful to remind users that specific research into CRM adoption has found that successful user adoption has been shown to improve both customer and employee satisfaction along with improved business performance. It is important that users believe the new CRM system will be not only a change but also a benefit. Sarin et al. defined the concept of *perceived impact of change* as "the degree to which a salesperson believes that the change will have a favorable effect on his or her well-being on the job."[10] Firms that embrace the stick side of the carrot/stick model of increasing adoption will find marginal CRM value if they cannot answer the fundamental question of how CRM helps both the individual and the organization. We will explore adoption and mechanisms to improve it in a later chapter.

Many organizations realize that replacing an old CRM system with a new one comes with opportunities for process improvement.

Contextual circumstances, however, such as monetary pressures resulting from the continuing use of the legacy product, lack of vendor support for the legacy product, or even the extreme frustration voiced by users as a result of poor features of the legacy product all may push organizations toward porting over one-for-one the functionality of the prior system without implementing improvements. While on the one hand users may appreciate the consistency in business process, they are still taxed with the responsibility to learn how to implement these processes in the new CRM system, which still presents all the challenges of learning to use any new system. The result is essentially: the same problems, but in different system. If business processes are poor in the legacy system, users will be unlikely to warm to the consistency argument. To complicate matters further, project sponsors and stakeholders may view the investment required by their subordinates—investment in participating in the requirements process, design reviews, acceptance testing, training, learning, and developing discipline to use the new system—as simply not worth it if they are also not realizing process improvements.

These circumstances encompass a scenario where the project is driven by constraints imposed on the Technology Division we noted earlier. In an attempt to gain user buy-in to the new CRM implementation, the division or project stakeholders might promise that—despite porting over functionality one-for-one now—they will revisit the implementation after they have completely moved off of the legacy system. Given all that is necessary to succeed at system modifications and enhancements—more training, change management, and increased time away from primary responsibilities to sit in more meetings with business analysts to hash out exactly what opportunities might exist for process improvement—it is not altogether surprising that the pledge to improve the system later might ring hollow. Once users are on the new system, they will perceive the next project to be focused on someone else and they will be left with the same problems on a new technology platform. The only real leverage firms have in this scenario is to implement a faster system and augment support resources to allow improved responses to user issues. Ultimately, this scenario underscores the reality that CRM does require a holistic enterprise approach and commitment to process improvement as a precondition to success.

Customer Centricity

Within the context of CRM literature, the notion of being "customer centric" is a common theme. It can be challenging to arrive at a clear definition of what it means for a culture to be customer centric or customer focused. A study by Chang, Park, and Chaiy in 2010 defined a customer-centric organizational culture as one that "encourages employees of the organization to consider customer relationships [as] a valuable asset and to utilize the tools to facilitate good [relationships] with customers (i.e., CRM technology) more actively."[3]

The idea is that by creating as complete a picture of a customer as possible, firms will be able to target sales and marketing efforts more effectively. The data that help firms to paint this picture may come from direct solicitation through sales calls, through analytics based on customers' past behaviors, and from external sources. Predictive models of customer purchasing behaviors are an extension of the effective capture and organization of a robust data set. These models seek to determine what product a customer will purchase next. Predictive models, though difficult to implement, are becoming increasingly popular given the results of several studies that have shown potential opportunities to engage in cross-selling and deepen existing relationships.

Customer centricity, in practical terms, could manifest itself as a kind of process discipline, such as entering a new business card promptly, inputting thorough meeting notes, and sending a note to the marketing team alerting them to the new contact. It is the difference between knowing what products a customer is buying and *why* he or she is buying them. Your product is a component of a customer's portfolio (in the broad sense). Once firms gain this understanding, they will have the ability to make more effective decisions.

Being customer centric implies a shift in focus onto the distribution channels of an organization: sales and marketing. Others who interface with customers include client service or customer care or customer relationship managers (a confusing term that we will only use once in this context). A successful CRM initiative will also remain cognizant that back-office functions can be viewed and shaped through a customer lens, such as in invoicing. Creating and sending an invoice is a task that involves a customer touch point. An invoice also sources customer data, which could be housed in a CRM system and notated as the system of record. This is one example underlying many firms' smart decisions to consider ERP as a component of their CRM strategy. An integration of a CRM system into an ERP system is a natural corollary. Some ERP systems are designed with the CRM application embedded as a module, which extends the notion of what ERP means and seeks to achieve. A customer-centric firm can be recognized by the degree to which it has shaped its strategy, processes, and technology around understanding, servicing, and retaining customers. In some firms such as professional services organizations, CRM might actually be—or can be configured to be—an ERP system in and of itself. Depending on the type of organization and contextual factors within each organization, this may or may not be the appropriate path to pursue. We will explore more about how CRM plays with other systems in a later chapter.

Chapter Summary

In this chapter, we have learned that achieving CRM success is the result of mastering a collection of functional, psychological, and technical factors. While functional factors such as poor business processes are certainly precursors to CRM failure, choices made during the technology implementation process have impacts on employee psychology, which can tank CRM initiatives just as much, if not more, as inefficient business processes. We have differentiated the conceptual notion of CRM from tangible CRM technology. We now understand the definitions of strategic, operational, analytical, and interactive CRM. We have explored the key drivers that cause firms to undertake CRM initiatives, which span both strategic and tactical goals. Some of these goals include increased revenue generation, quantifying the specific value of customer relationships, and maintaining competitive advantage. Finally, we defined customer centricity and identified it as the key orientation that firms must adopt in order to be successful.

References

1. Hendricks, K. B., Singhal, V. R., & Stratman, J. K. (2007). The impact of enterprise systems on corporate performance: A study of ERP, SCM, and CRM system implementations. *Journal of Operations Management* 25, 65–82.

2. Liu, A. Z., Liu, H., & Xu, S. X. (2013). How do competitive environments moderate CRM value? *Decision Support Systems 56*, 462–473.

3. Chang, W., Park, J. E., & Chaiy, S. (2010). How does CRM technology transform into organizational performance? A mediating role of marketing capability. *Journal of Business Research 63*, 849–855.

4. Saxena, R. P., & Khandelwal, P. K. (2011). Exploring customer perception and behavior towards CRM practices in banking sector: An empirical analysis. *The International Journal of Interdisciplinary Social Sciences 5(9)*, 375–391.

5. Kippley, T., & Schneider, B. (2016, February 18). CRM practitioners—Rightpoint (S. J. Kinnett, Interviewer).

6. Baker, D. S., & Delpechitre, D. (2013). Collectivistic and individualistic performance expectancy in the utilization of sales automation technology in an international field sales setting. *Journal of Personal Selling & Sales Management 33(3)*, 277–288.

7. Ang, L., & Buttle, F. (2006). CRM software applications and business performance. *Database of Marketing & Customer Strategy Management 14*, 4–16.

8. Anonymous. (2016, January 12–13). Making CRM successful—CRM practitioner interview (S. J. Kinnett, Interviewer).

9. Lidwell, W., Holden, K., & Butler, J. (2010). *Universal Principles of Design*. Beverly, MA: Rockport.

10. Sarin, S., Sego, T., Kohli, A. K., & Challagalla, G. (2010). Characteristics that enhance training effectiveness in implementing technological change in sales strategy: A field-based exploratory study. *Journal of Personal Selling & Sales Management 30(2)*, 143–156.

2
SALESPERSON RESISTANCE

The psychology of the salesperson is paramount to our understanding of why customer relationship management (CRM) often fails and how to make it successful. CRM is a philosophy driven by marketing and sales management rather than from the frontline sales force, folks who are already customer focused—they are the ones visiting offices, making follow-up calls, signing Christmas cards, and memorizing birthdays. When marketing and the executive offices started educating them about being customer centric, no doubt many must have scratched their heads at the existence of such a term.

Some practitioners have noticed a theme surrounding user attitudes about CRM and other technology solutions. Salespeople perceive themselves—by and large—as being bad at technology. We have heard this sentiment expressed directly and implicitly. To the latter, we have often fielded support calls from folks expressing a sense of despair. They first criticize the CRM (not unjustifiably), but by the end of the call, they sigh and admit that their challenge resulted from a core lack of technology understanding. As it regards professional development and time in the industry, "a salesperson's experience was found to be negatively related to a salesperson's technology orientation."[1] We must take care that these results do not become a prescription for ageism: discrimination based on age. It is illegal and unethical. There does appear to be come correlation, however, to a salesperson's age and his technology prowess. Younger folks are more likely to have had contextual exposure to technology and technological innovation, so it would be naive for organizations not to be cognizant of the demographic composition of their salespeople. More experienced salespeople should not be discouraged. At least some firms have probably taken the advice above and do evaluate potential recruits based on factors including technology prowess. By being aware of this reality, more experienced salespeople can take initiative to improve their technology skills to be competitive in this evolving sales environment.

Resistance and Cynicism

A study by Selander and Henfridsson in 2012 suggests that CRM systems do not typically provide ample opportunities for compromise when user goals are at odds with management goals or information technology (IT) restrictions. As a result, they see CRM implementations as environments highly conducive to resistance and cynicism. They described cynicism—in this context—as "a combination of cognitive distance, negative affect, and seeing through espoused claims."[2]

Resistance begins when users juxtapose the impact of CRM against prior operational conditions. These initial conditions are the perceptions that individuals or groups have about "established work routines, power relationships or the internal organizational structure."[2] Users may have criticisms of the system itself—features, user interface, and speed—along with criticisms of the implications of the system in the ways it could impact work and power structures. An example of this second type of criticism is the resistance that inevitably presents when salespeople sacrifice anonymity for visibility and potential public scrutiny and shaming. In either scenario, users will begin distancing themselves from the objects of their concerns. Selandar and Henfridsson suggest that the distancing process seeks to "create an inner space of dignity and integrity, insulated from the organizational environment."[2]

Negative affect presents itself as irony, sarcasm, or mockery and is also presented discursively through gossiping, skepticism, and storytelling. Users in this position will be especially sensitive to management mistakes and inconsistencies, and feel compelled to refute these claims to others. Negative affect is easily transferred to others in the same environment. One of the most insidious manifestations of user resistance occurs when users turn upon their own colleagues who are CRM advocates. We will later discuss at length the importance of including salespeople in the implementation process to ensure buy-in and generate advocates who can be used to train others and evangelize the system. Selander and Henfridsson noted that not only members of the implementation team—such as the Technology Division and external implementation partner—but anyone who advocates for the system, such as super users, may also face resistance.

Identifying these types of behaviors can help firms gauge where they stand in their CRM initiative in a way that recording the number of phone calls and meetings per salesperson per month could never do. All the while, we must remember that these challenges, however daunting, are virtually unavoidable. According to Baker and Delpechitre (2013), salespeople are a user base notorious for being "among the most technophobic and resistant of all white-collar workers...."[3] Chalmeta in 2006 concluded that all of these difficulties result from the lack of awareness of CRM's importance and benefits, which can be realized with effective relationship management. A few mechanisms to improve awareness include enlisting top management support, creating super users, or deploying technical evangelists throughout the organization.

The concept of user cynicism underscores the importance of focusing on technology usability as a key factor in driving positive CRM outcomes. With so much emphasis in CRM literature of culture and strategy, it can be very tempting to allow the pendulum to swing too far in that direction leading to costly technological compromises. In one study examining the implementation of a packaged CRM system—despite management focus on driving customer-centric business practices—"the new system soon became an object of resistance, not least because of its significance for customer service practices."[2] In other words, forcing folks to reorient themselves to a given paradigm and subsequently providing them with inferior tools to execute on that paradigm is a recipe for failure.

When users return to spreadsheets or other CRM substitutes, Selander and Henfridsson suggest system accuracy to be a direct antecedent to this flight from CRM. In particular, their study demonstrated that users "feared the lack of system support and the considerable overtime required to handle the ever-increasing number of unsolved customer cases."[2] This anxiety has real impacts, when increasing volumes of customer data are maintained outside of the CRM. In the CRM space, the capture and maintenance of data outside of the CRM system of record is a significant risk to the firm.

Control

Another component of salesperson resistance is the lack of control they feel about CRM. While they may know on some level that CRM can provide a number of benefits to a firm and even to the salespeople themselves, they resent the way it is forced on them by sales management. To that end, we should remain mindful that our primary users had this methodology, these requirements, forced upon them. At the most basic level, we should not expect the presence of this technology to yield any positive emotion from a salesperson. It is all too easy for firms to forget that "the salesperson is the 'internal customer' of any CRM system, whose needs and beliefs must be understood, managed, and eventually satisfied, if performance improvements are to be realized."[4] Many of the recommendations in this book are designed to minimize salesperson resistance. Especially in firms that have not engaged the frontline sales force sufficiently, salesperson resistance may be justified. This theme extends to the implementation of enterprise technology more broadly, a point underscored in an essay by Arussy, who noted that users' systems are purchased without their consent, buy-in, or excitement. This does not exactly predispose users to be cooperative, and our ability to succeed in our CRM initiatives without users' cooperation is reduced as a result. One potential point to mitigate this challenge would be involving some portion of users in the software selection process.

An important reality often unacknowledged is that salespeople tend to be sensitive, emotional, and—to paraphrase one salesperson's self-assessment—"coin operated." Or, put more formally, they are "the revenue generators, and when faced with an opportunity to close a deal, they can't stumble."[5] Disruptions to a sales person's daily processes, such as poor technology implementations, managerial overreach, and micromanagement, will induce a visceral response. This is a markedly different paradigm than one would find in the services fields, where poor CRM technology and processes would result in operational inefficiencies and some potentially awkward customer service interactions, but would—in most cases—not result in a salaried employee taking home a smaller paycheck.

Perceived Goal Conflict

To make matters even more complicated, sometimes sales management's goals for CRM are in direct conflict—or are perceived to be in direct conflict—with CRM users' goals. One study highlighted a key sales management benefit of implementing CRM, noting that "if the accuracy of the system is credible, the 'chain of evidence' will show who (salesperson) is doing what, when, based on what information, and in this environment of full disclosure, accountability will be… transparent."[6] Sounds horrible. Do other departments face this level of scrutiny?

Another very telling finding from a study by Clark, Rocco, and Bush in 2007 noted that "sales managers were found to be more likely to perceive productivity or efficiency gains from [Sales force Automation] technology than were those actually *using* the technology, the sales force."[1] Complicating matters further, the sales force almost universally viewed the CRM system as primarily a micromanagement tool. Tim Kippley of Rightpoint Consulting provided some clarity on why sales managers are often so interested in CRM, noting,

> They want visibility. That is, the idea that they can start at a high level and see how the health of the business is doing and drill as deep as they want. Giving them control to view things at whatever level they want to see it [is another selling point]. They want to see their version of the truth. They say "I want to see my region—how product X is selling. Which accounts are at risk?"[7]

These goals—especially when presented to those salespeople whose orientation is more toward what could be called the "art of sales" rather than the "science of sales"—are admittedly at odds with nurturing relationships and bringing home commissions. What can we do to bridge this gap? As Schneider and Kippley of Rightpoint Consulting suggest, one of the most powerful ways to do so is to answer the implicit question on every salesperson's mind: "what's in it for me?" Failing to answer this question has the potential to tank even the well-designed CRM initiative.

Perceptions on Necessity

Another challenging truth further compounds the adoption challenge, which is that salespeople themselves do not really *need* a CRM system. As Kippley noted previously, salespeople have been selling long before the Information Age, and—for some—a spreadsheet is just as good as a clunky CRM, if not better. Salespeople know to a large degree that they could survive without a CRM system and that it may or may not benefit them to use one. Indeed, there is empirical evidence that "automating the sales force does not necessarily lead to desirable consequences."[8] Salespeople may well perceive that a CRM system is getting in the way of their success, and in some cases, it might be.

A good CRM system could certainly provide benefits unavailable via more rudimentary tools, but a poor one might not. Drawing upon our examination of CRM as an inhibitor to achieving desired commissions, a study in 2005 noted that the "implementation of SFA technology could create unreasonable work demands to be placed on salespeople. These demands usually include devoting additional time for learning about the technology, spending more time using the technology on the job, and troubleshooting technological problems."[8] All of these realities translate to fewer client visits, which has a very real connection to successful sales and thus lower commissions and frustrated salespeople. The moment CRM gets in the way of someone's ability to make money, the adoption challenge becomes exponentially more complicated.

One veteran salesperson noted that with so many options available to sales management and the CRM practitioner, the risk of bloated, useless functionality becomes more and more prevalent as technology improves. When it comes to implementing so-called features, he noted, "just because you can doesn't mean you should." When CRM systems introduce unnecessary overhead and complexity to salespeople, who in a given day may perform a variety of tasks, including creating new contacts, updating an opportunity, and preparing pitches and price quotes, an understandable frustration exists that the system purported to help with these processes actually provides operational challenges as salespeople attempt to navigate the system's complexities. Beasty in 2006 noted that part of the problem is that "salespeople are forced to do too much administrative work."[5] As organizations and practitioners proceed identifying functional requirements, they could benefit from checking themselves when implementing administrative functionality for salespeople and consider removing that functionality from a salesperson profile and assigning the responsibility to, for example, an administrative assistant. Data stewardship considerations are also important to examine in this context, which we will explore in a later chapter in greater depth.

This collective theme—the disconnect between satisfaction by end users versus stakeholders and decision makers—underscores the importance of technology quality. We are already working from behind when it comes to adoption. The mandate for use—in the eyes of the primary users, salespeople—is almost entirely driven upon others' goals. We might shrug and wipe a false tear from the eye and think about all of the problems we have in our own roles—all of which are probably valid and should be addressed—but such a posture will not allow us to be successful. All business units should always have strong technology, but it is in the CRM space where we see the largest divergence between the importance of stability and usability vis-à-vis the actual quality of deployed software. The extant literature points often to technology quality as a cause of salesperson resistance. Data quality is a component of poor technology and is another problem ripe to alienate our users. Since poor data quality in the CRM space translates to awkward conversations and potential client loss, it is not so difficult to have empathy for the salesperson's plight. As we often see in organizational analysis, expectation management—about both benefits and specific expectations of usage—plays an important role in inoculating CRM advocates from unnecessary political headaches.

Implications of Role Conflict

Minimizing salesperson stress and thus improving odds for adoption are dependent on how well CRM becomes part of a salesperson's daily process as opposed to being an adjunct tool that receives attention only during the performance of mandatory functions. For example, salespeople who still build their call lists in spreadsheets rather than within CRM have clearly not allowed CRM to meld into their daily process. A study in 2005 underscored this point, noting that "the degree to which salespeople perceive the task of integrating SFA technology into their routine activities as complex gives rise to feelings of technology-related role ambiguity and role conflict,"[8] which in turn contributes directly to stress and resistance.

This same study also provides instructive insights surrounding support of CRM systems. We will explore the development and implementation of a CRM support model in a later chapter, but it is important to note that CRM support is absolutely critical to CRM success. To that end, the study's authors believe that

> when faced with situations where trying to use SFA technology increases demands on the job and adequate support is not provided, salespeople are more likely to spend effort on issues with which they are more familiar (e.g., calling on customers, following up on leads) than on integrating SFA technology into their work routines.[8]

The longer a salesperson is absent from utilizing the CRM system, the more likely he or she will be to adopt other methods to manage his or her sales process, such as offline spreadsheets. A salesperson in such situations on a chronic basis will almost certainly not adopt extended-use functionality and will engage only with core functionality required as an absolute condition of his employment. Entering call and meeting notes is one example of a function considered to be mandatory at many firms. We will explore the intricacies of extended and postadoptive use later in this book.

Extending role conflict and ambiguity further, it is important to remember that salespeople are under constant scrutiny and threat of replacement if they do not meet sales numbers. This creates uncertainty about the permanence of their roles. It is also unclear on what priorities they should focus. In a basic example—entirely outside of CRM—organizations that require extensive administrative overhead from salespeople may create conflicting demands because these activities take time away from sales.

The study discussed above by Rangarajan, Jones, and Chin also suggests that any technical implementation places a burden by requiring time to learn these systems at a time when no other responsibilities are removed: quotas are unaltered, compensation remains commission based. The study suggests that role conflict "perhaps arises when sales-people perceive the time they spend on learning to integrate the tech-nology could be better spent with customers or doing other required duties."[8] Such role conflict is exacerbated when support resources are insufficient. We will explore effective means to provide system sup-port to mitigate this risk factor in a later chapter.

Managing Resistance

As we can see, the process of managing salesperson resistance requires diligence on multiple fronts, particularly in the context of providing clarity on expectations and roles. The successful integration of CRM technology and process into the salesperson's daily routine is a direct precursor to CRM success. Training programs to ensure basic sys-tem competence are useful. Additionally, managers may benefit from communicating concise, unambiguous guidelines and procedures. Rangarajan, Jones, and Chin suggest that the content of these guide-lines should explicitly state

> (1) the reasons for using the SFA technology, (2) the possible change in work activities expected from salespeople due to SFA technology, (3) information regarding sharing of private customer information with the rest of the organization, (4) the scope for monitoring activities of salespeople, and (5) changing expectations on the job as a result of SFA technology.[8]

Note that these guidelines go well beyond communication of manda-tory usage and functional training. Recommendations 3 and 4 dis-cuss information sharing and monitoring. These points are especially useful in combating the resentment that arises from salespeople who prefer not to share information about their customer interactions. Essentially, these recommendations speak to the criticality of not just providing clarity on how to use the system but also how the system impacts a salesperson's work life and daily processes. It also suggests, as other studies have, that CRM is not an isolated or adjunct piece of technology, but indeed a strategy, process, and essential technical component of daily operations.

Chapter Summary

In this chapter, we have explored salesperson psychology and resistance leading to an understanding that salespeople themselves must be sold on CRM systems, which are often management or marketing initiatives that are undertaken without the salesperson's consent. We now understand that CRM causes significant consternation for salespeople, particularly as it surrounds the definition of their roles, management's expectations on CRM usage, and information sharing and access. Salespeople are also often unconvinced that CRM is even necessary, especially very tenured salespeople who can point to an era where CRM technology was absent.

We now see that understanding how CRM will impact a salesperson's daily routines and practices is as important as making sure that they have received adequate functional training on the CRM product, as well as on technology, more broadly in order to increase their technical literacy. Management can benefit from unambiguous communication that clearly outlines the reasons for using the technology, the impact of using the system to existing work activities, the organization's information sharing and monitoring policies, and what impact the CRM processes will have on managers' expectations of employees. In the next chapter, we will explore important facets of organizational culture and readiness to implement a CRM initiative.

References

1. Clark, P., Rocco, R. A., & Bush, A. J. (2007). Sales force automation systems and sales force productivity: Critical issues and research agenda. *Journal of Relationship Marketing 6(2)*, 67–87.
2. Selander, L., & Henfridsson, O. (2012). Cynicism as user resistance in IT implementation. *Information Systems Journal 22*, 289–312.
3. Baker, D. S., & Delpechitre, D. (2013). Collectivistic and individualistic performance expectancy in the utilization of sales automation technology in an international field sales setting. *Journal of Personal Selling & Sales Management 33(3)*, 277–288.
4. Avlonitis, G. J., & Panagopoulos, N. G. (2005). Antecedents and consequences of CRM technology acceptance in the sales force. *Industrial Marketing Management 34*, 355–368.
5. Beasty, C. (2006, February). Why sales teams should use CRM. *Customer Relationship Management 31–34*.

6. Peterson, R. M., Rodriguez, M., & Krishnan, V. (2011). CRM and sales pipeline management: Empirical results for managing opportunities. *The Marketing Management Journal 21(1)*, 60–70.
7. Kippley, T., & Schneider, B. (2016, February 18). CRM practitioners—Rightpoint (S. J. Kinnett, Interviewer).
8. Rangarajan, D., Jones, E., & Chin, W. (2005). Impact of sales force automation on technology-related stress, effort, and technology usage among salespeople. *Industrial Marketing Management 34*, 345–354.

3

CULTURE OF SUCCESS

Implementing a successful customer relationship management (CRM) initiative is similar to growing a plant. A number of conditions must be met in order for the plant to take root and grow (such as soil, sunlight, and water). Collectively, these three preconditions form what can be called the plant's environment. So, too, a firm's culture is a collection of components. A deficiency in any of these components impacts the culture as a whole, just as nutrient-deficient soil, inadequate water, or insufficient sunlight will prevent a plant from surviving and thriving. Defining organizational culture is to some degree a subjective task. In a 2011 study, Garrido-Moreno and Padilla-Melendez, however, nicely characterize culture as aspects relating to top management leadership, cross-functional alignment, organizational structure, and human resource management. We might extend this definition to include the qualities a firm values such as prioritizing employee development, promoting wellness and focusing on diversity initiatives.

A CRM strategy is born directly from organizational culture, and it requires myriad changes to organizational structures, operational procedures, support processes, and top management commitments. The criticality of top management support, buy-in, and commitment cannot be overstated given the sheer volume of studies that highlight its importance. While there are many important factors to achieving CRM success, top management support always finds its way to the top. While we will discuss the importance of management support in greater detail later in this chapter, we should first define what we mean by success in the CRM game.

Success Defined

Measuring the success of information systems (IS) in enabling the success of an overall strategy has long been a topic of discussion in the academic and business communities. DeLone and McLean's 1992 study on IS success continues to be the seminal work on the topic, with many journal articles referencing it as the foundation of incremental research. DeLone and McLean's success model—as explained by T. H. Roh et al. in 2005—measures IS success in six categories: "system quality, information quality, system use, individual impact, organizational impact, and user satisfaction."[1] Ifinedo used a slightly modified set of criteria in his 2011 study:

- System quality
- Information quality
- Individual impact
- Workgroup impact
- Organizational impact[2]

This list excludes system use and user satisfaction, but it includes workgroup impact. Enterprise resource planning (ERP) systems and CRM systems are often broken out separately in the literature, but we will find throughout our examination of CRM success factors and practices that many of them are analogous to those for ERP. In one sense, CRM can be considered a subset of ERP, as it is reflected in some vendor-built ERP software packages. CRM can also be considered as its own initiative, which requires collaboration with and system integration into ERP.

At first glance, it may seem that the first four items in our list are mediating factors on the last: organizational impact. In Ifinedo's study, however, organizational impact is characterized as to what degree decision-making processes and customer service have been improved.

Elsewhere in this text, we will explore the importance of gaining user buy-in by "selling" them on the benefits of the CRM by phrasing it in terms that demonstrate the benefit to them. The impact on salespeople and other end users can be defined as *individual impact*: the ability to operate productively and make better decisions. Another component of success is *workgroup impact*—also known as intraorganizational impact—which is assessed by "improved interdepartmental coordination, communication, and productivity."[2] The aged paradigm of salespeople as lone wolves becomes relevant at this point in the discussion. The less focus a firm places on collaboration, a key factor to influencing workgroup impact, the greater a firm's propensity toward organic knowledge sharing—the natural dissemination of knowledge among colleagues via normal oral or written conversational channels—will be diminished. This phenomenon is an example of what Iriana, Buttle, and Ang called *suboptimal organizational behavior*, using as their example "the propensity of sales people to resist making customer knowledge available to colleagues."[3]

The notion of CRM yielding organizational benefits outside of financial performance is corroborated in a 2005 study, which concluded that CRM initiatives "influence profitability indirectly through [the] efficiency and customer satisfaction [paths], which in turn fosters profitability."[1] Their findings were empirically supported 2 years later by research suggesting that reducing time spent on non-selling tasks would be an important gain and an appropriate measure of success. Ahearne et al. note that "technology [systems] should reduce time spent on nonselling tasks, such as scheduling sales calls, updating customer records, compiling sales reports, and assembling market information,"[4] which are all examples of efficiency gains. This latter study, while robust, does not examine the particulars of the technology they are measuring. In other words, we would posit that the above assertion is true, provided that the sales technology itself is sufficiently usable.

Firms are keen to receive every possible benefit from the implementation of CRM strategy and CRM technology, and rightfully so given the large capital investment required for such initiatives. Since CRM is not just a piece of technology but also an enterprise strategy, folks may be looking for their initiative to yield benefits beyond operational efficiencies and the—admittedly vague—notion of organizational impact. Since the aim of any business is to make money, the question of whether CRM will translate to profits is often top of mind. If a case presents itself where you have high CRM adoption but low return, consider the possibility that the CRM may be creating a number of operational efficiencies that do not translate to revenue gains. This is not uncommon and should not be viewed as a failure of the CRM. Operational improvement may take years to manifest as revenue gains, and operational improvement may yield benefits in ancillary ways including employee retention. That is, employees with efficient operating procedures will be happier than those who are bogged down with redundancy, slow systems, or unnecessary administrative overhead.

Voicing your intention to measure the success of a CRM implementation is a necessary precondition to the implementation process. Identifying measurements surrounding, for example, postadoptive use could be conceived throughout the implementation. Firms would be best suited by finding means to measure adoption or efficiency before attempting to make the jump straight to measuring revenue gains at the expense of other important benefits that can result from CRM. One consultant noted in a 2016 interview that measuring the success of CRM implementations is often not understood by those embarking on CRM initiatives. He noted that throughout the past decade, he has found a number of clients who are totally unfocused on measuring success at all, through revenue or otherwise. Often consumed with intense focus to get the project across the finish line and then move on with their lives, organizations may neglect implementing measurements of adoption. As our consultant noted, "if you're not getting traction on user adoption, you've spent a lot of effort building something with a short shelf life."[5]

Organizational Cultural Structures

While we realize that organizational culture encompasses a vast conglomeration of factors, some research has revealed insights into the impact of what might be called a cultural structure on CRM initiatives. Most firms can be classified as—in this paradigm—aligning with one of three culture structures: adhocracy, hierarchy, or clan culture. Given that organizational psychology is part of our thesis about the factors that need to be understood to master CRM, cultural understanding flows naturally from psychological understanding. We will now examine each of the above types of cultural structures, their characteristics, and their relationships to CRM initiatives.

Adhocracy

The adhocracy organizational structure refers to a nimble organization, drawing from the Latin words *ad hoc*, which implies lack of repeatability or suggests something special that must be addressed directly. Adhocracy-based solutions are not largely leveraged from previous experience. Most start-up companies would begin as adhocracies.

To that end, it is the maturity of an organization that can cause decay of adhocracy culture and a morphing into hierarchy culture. Organizational maturity does not, however, causally predict this metamorphosis. When entrepreneurially oriented employees see red tape, decreased flexibility, and consistently standardized (read: not creative) solutions, they may choose to find a new company that better suits their personalities.

To that end, sometimes great leaders in an adhocracy culture are poor leaders in a hierarchy culture. Consider the serial entrepreneur who upon finding that his or her corporation no longer requires daily innovation decides to start a new one. In an adhocracy, "the leaders themselves are considered risk takers and innovators, who believe that the major task of management is to foster entrepreneurship, creativity, and activity 'on the edge'. The glue that holds the organization together is widespread commitment to experimentation and innovation."[3] Adhocracies are primarily interested in expansion and growth. They measure success by quantity and quality of innovation, and the culture is typically oriented toward freedom and individual empowerment.

Hierarchy Culture

The next form of organizational culture we can examine in the context of its orientation toward innovation such as CRM is the hierarchy culture. "Mature" organizations have typically become hierarchy cultures, visible by highly formalized procedures. In some ways, a hierarchy culture might seem to be the most evolved form of a company, yet the plethora of American—and no doubt other—employees who wrinkle their noses at the prospect of working for large multinational corporations in lieu of agile start-ups reminds us that facets of hierarchy culture may be more valued by the organization's management than by its employees.

A hierarchy culture places its focus on continuity and groupthink. Effective leaders are measured by their success in making processes more efficient and their ability to juggle many resources and initiatives simultaneously. Lone wolf creative thinkers may find themselves stifled in such cultures. As it pertains to success, hierarchy culture measures dependability, timeliness, and cost. In the context of CRM implementations, hierarchy cultures believe it is important that "business rules and processes are formalized before technology is rolled out."[3]

Clan Culture

Private companies, partnerships, and family businesses are perhaps the most susceptible contexts to the cultural notion of a clan. Clan cultures can be identified by their "shared values and goals, cohesion, participation, and a sense of 'we-ness'...."[3] Clan culture—for employees—sounds wonderful. This culture prioritizes employee development and internal initiatives over external success, and it evaluates itself by how much it can do for its employees. Clans likely will be less interested in pushing the envelope and driving innovation unless it has a clear operational benefit to employees. The prevalence of teamwork in clan culture is useful for CRM success, but Iriana, Buttle, and Ang in their 2013 research noted that "other clan attributes impede the achievement of CRM financial success."[3]

Analysis

As we noted above, the teamwork attribute of clan culture cannot make up for other cultural shortcomings, which was noted by Iriana, Buttle, and Ang in their 2013 study of these cultural structures on CRM success. They found that "adhocracy culture has the strongest positive association with good CRM financial outcomes. Clan culture has a significant negative association with good CRM financial outcomes."[3]

Hierarchy cultures have the potential to realize benefits from CRM, but these benefits are largely dependent on how much of the adhocracy culture a hierarchical culture can tolerate. While a hierarchy culture benefits in its commitment to operational efficiency, it will need to become more comfortable with risk and innovation in order to realize maximum CRM success, which "may involve changes in organizational leadership towards one that stresses creativity and innovation, and values risk taking."[3] Hierarchy cultures can sometimes cut the tallest blade of grass and prefer that folks adhere to process and bureaucracy over innovation, whereas "in adhocracies, employees are encouraged to act innovatively to satisfy customers. They will be empowered to build long-term profitable customer relationships, and rewarded for doing so."[3]

We can see that—in and of themselves—each of these three organizational cultures has benefits and limitations. Each culture can find reasons to implement CRM. An adhocracy, the most natural candidate, will be drawn to CRM as an innovation that can drive customer acquisition and advance the firm's position. Hierarchy cultures can appreciate the operational efficiency, risk management, and protection from embarrassing client interactions that CRM can provide. Even clan cultures could be influenced by a CRM's benefit to employee satisfaction through streamlined processes, elimination of redundancy, and—ideally—a pleasing technology experience. Ultimately, however, "regardless of whether the CRM system is easy to use or compatible with existing systems, having an organizational culture conducive to the achievement of good CRM outcomes (adhocracy, hierarchy) is still the most important driver."[3]

The Learning Enterprise

CRM plays an important role in the capture and dissemination of information to contribute to organizational intelligence. Some studies have examined firm culture through the lens of organizational learning. The results of these studies suggest that a sophisticated CRM system—coupled with organizational culture that encourages learning and innovation—will drive an increase in salesperson knowledge. When evaluating that notion, Park, Kim, Dubinsky, and Lee in their 2010 study concluded that "it is not the technology per se but rather the individual learning that occurs through, and as a result of, its utilization that ultimately creates superior performance."[6]

As a result of this realization, it makes sense that firm leadership and management should undertake initiatives to build a learning culture into their sales force. This culture should "inculcate in sales personnel the importance of their collecting and using market information. Emphasis could be placed on how such information can assist salespeople in tailoring their customer interactions, ultimately contributing to improved relationships with their customers...."[6] Studies have shown that senior salespeople are more likely to solicit, process, and utilize market information, and as such, they would be in a prime position to educate more junior folks about its importance. In practice, "this could be done through a mentoring system or through part of the formal training program for junior salespeople, where the more experienced salespeople serve as ad hoc trainers."[6] The fundamentals of using the CRM system should also be a top training priority to ensure that technical illiteracy does not persist as a barrier to use as noted in the previous chapter.

Organizational Readiness and Barriers to Entry

Perfection is the enemy of action, but some studies have shown just about everything needs to be in top working order before implementing a CRM strategy. Multiple components have been found to be important precursors to successful CRM implementation, including changes in structure, incentives, or training as well as business units' plans, goals, and alignment to the Technology Division. In a 2006 study, Chelmeta provides tough love in his blunt advice to organizations considering implementing CRM or other innovations, noting the harsh reality that "the fact that a company is already functioning and has satisfactory financial results does not mean it is efficient, nor does it mean that it has its objectives and responsibilities properly defined."[7] This underscores the difference between adequate functions and optimal functions. Given that many CRMs do not translate into firm financial performance for at least 3 years, if ever, it, therefore, remains necessary to define other measures of performance.

Organizational Climate

An organization's climate plays an important role in achieving CRM success. We can think of climate as the implementation of culture. Climate refers primarily to employees' perceptions about office procedures and practices, as well as perceptions about reward systems and expectations for advancement. In a 2002 study of organizational climate, Pullig, Maxham III, and Hair evaluated a number of factors that they theorized could create a climate where CRM could flourish. Of all factors examined, they found that the most important factors were "(1) training; (2) encouragement; (3) facilitative leadership; and (4) organizational support."[8] We will now examine each of these factors in greater depth.

Training   The extant literature has shown training to be the most important factor of an organization's climate that must be mastered to achieve CRM success. Without training, users cannot possibly be counted upon to learn the system more than the most basic functions they need to fulfill core management requirements. The absence of training would set a terrible tone upon the CRM initiative, indicating that management thought little of the project. Pullig et al. in their study suggest that SFA (analogous to CRM for these purposes) training should provide both general computing skills and SFA system competence. General computing skills are important to avoid having a staff who is uncomfortable with computer technology. Beyond general computer literacy, specific training must provide users with the necessary knowledge and understanding of the SFA system. Pullig et al.'s findings on the importance of core technical literacy are as applicable as they were in 2002. Despite an ever-growing portion of the workforce possessing technical competence, a large segment still lacks basic understanding and governing principles of computer systems. This makes any effort at training this population doomed to failure. We will explore training further in a future chapter.

Encouragement   Pullig et al. in their study suggest that encouragement is the second most important climate factor to provide strong antecedents to CRM success. This encouragement manifests in the way of lessening or removing barriers to use the system coupled with incentives to use the system. The importance of executive support is another example of encouragement and perhaps one of the most powerful. Encouragement cannot be a point in time solution, but rather an ongoing reality within firms striving for CRM success. Both trainers and technical evangelists are good candidates to supply the requisite encouragement. We will explore both of these functions in later chapters.

Facilitative Leadership   Facilitative leadership was ranked slightly lower than encouragement, though the two are certainly related. Facilitative leadership is a leadership style focused on personnel development, and it supports learning and encourages an inquisitive organizational climate. Such leaders are focused on cross-functional information sharing. They are strong communicators and motivators.

Pullig, Maxham III, and Hair concluded that this type of leadership is necessary to create a climate that is coordinated in its efforts to improve customer service. This focus on cross-functional transfer of information and creation of a learning organization is corroborated in our examination of employee alignment. Facilitative leaders achieve success through both words and actions. A successful CRM climate would "ensure that organization members have appropriate skills, sufficient support, and an atmosphere of esprit de corps in using the SFA system."[8] This point is strongly related to the importance of top management support, which is explored throughout this book and which the extant literature has largely found to be a key risk factor for CRM implementation failure.

Organizational Support   The final variable found to be significant in Pullig et al.'s 2002 study was organizational support, defined as "the extent to which technical problems and user questions are handled properly."[8] The definition is broad. We will explore specific facets of implementation, including the implementation of an effective support model, which will ensure that organizational support is robust. Organizational support includes strong technical support, training, and responsiveness to user inquiry. Lack of support increases frustration, breeds cynicism, and decreases adoption.

Selected Key Risk Factors

So much of the literature on CRM focuses on the failures and the potential for failure. The purpose of this section is to understand key themes that have caused problems for firms out of the gate so that these problems can be mitigated before a CRM project begins. When considering risks and potential barriers to entry, we should ensure that our focus remains on tangible and common challenges. We should not invent reasons not to implement or enhance CRM. There will never be a perfect time to undertake any process to attain a large goal, and implementing CRM is no exception. Analysis of barriers to entry should be taken as a guide and not a mandate to paralyze decision-making.

Researchers in Iran conducted a thorough study in 2013 that included a comprehensive survey of CRM risk literature. They concluded in the study that stakeholder turnover and top management attrition comprise, collectively, the primary risk factor for CRM implementation failure. The researchers also noted "managers' incorrect cognition of CRM and its operational and strategic benefits"[9] as key contributors to failures in CRM. This incorrect cognition plays a significant role in influencing subsequent top management support. These researchers found that ambiguity around CRM goals and a lack of perception of the organizational culture and environment round out the top user concerns. The complete list of the factors they examined is shown in the following:

1. Insufficient perception of the organization and environment
2. Immaturity of [the organization] in [information technology and information systems]
3. Weakness in communication infrastructures and unfavorable quality of internal communications
4. Lack of customer and change-oriented culture
5. Weakness in customer strategy
6. Weakness in customer interaction strategy
7. Weakness in brand strategy
8. Weakness in value creation strategy
9. Lack of organizational structure and [a] customer-centric [organization]
10. Change in stakeholders and top management
11. Managers' incorrect cognition of CRM and its operational and strategic benefits
12. Absence of the CRM project in the company's strategy plan
13. Insufficient funding for CRM
14. Ambiguity in aims of CRM implementation
15. Interfunctional conflict
16. Weakness in selecting the most suitable technology
17. Weakness in implementation technology and project management
18. Lack of strategic coordination between HRM and CRM
19. Lack of incentive systems for encouraging customers to interact actively with the organization
20. Neglecting the customer['s] trust and privacy
21. Not involving final users in designing the CRM solution

22. Not employing interfunctional criteria of performance evaluation
23. Not employing process-oriented criteria of performance
24. Weakness of feedback system in [the] correction of strategies and processes
25. Lack of benchmarking of similar organizations to define criteria of performance management and comparing outcomes.[9]

We have already begun to explore the importance of firm culture on CRM success. We will now expand this discussion to encompass additional facets of organizational culture and their respective contributions to the CRM implementation and adoption processes. A 2003 study found that "more than half of CRM failures have been blamed on the challenges of company politics, inertia and implementing organizational change—not software and not budgets."[10] We should not discount the role of software and budgets. Effective technology and resourcing are necessary but not sufficient conditions to achieving CRM success. Budgets are a strategic factor resulting from the organization's posture toward resource allocation. In today's landscape, firms should be prepared to spend a million or more to achieve the CRM results they want.

One study conducted in 2001—aged, yes, but interesting given one of our core assertions—noted that "overly expensive investment in technology—both software and hardware—is cited as a significant cause of CRM's failure to deliver value."[11] In a 2010 study, Battor and Battor supported this conclusion, positing that "allocating resources is likely to be a helpful but not sufficient condition for innovation success. It may be possible for firms to fail even when they have resources...."[12] While certainly throwing money at something is no guarantee of success, let us not forget that often we get what we pay for. One potential conclusion to be drawn here is that large CRM cost expenditures may be correlated with overly complicated implementations. A recurring theme throughout this text is the reality that CRM only succeeds when it is kept simple and users understand and embrace its benefits. The investments we propose to technology may not be so costly when weighed against their benefits. Later in this book, we will examine CRM software strategy and implementation details in depth, with the notion of *simplicity* being one of our key principles. In a 2012 study, Chung, Hsu, Tsai, Huang, and Tsai confirmed the importance of keeping the Technology Division actively involved, noting that such involvement "significantly and positively influence[s] the implementation of CRM activities; a higher implementation level of CRM activities significantly and positively influences business performance."[13]

Top Management Support

Elmuti, Jia, and Gray noted in their 2009 study that top management support is "perhaps the most important strategic factor that needs to be present [for successful CRM implementations]."[14] The role of top management support is a strong recurring theme throughout the CRM literature, and its importance cannot be overstated, primarily because of the strong influence of firm culture and strategy to CRM success—both factors heavily influenced by top management. One role of management is to advocate for and fund CRM initiatives. The former is necessary to rally users via management's political and compensatory influences, and the latter to enable users via education and effective headcount allocation. Tim Kippley highlighted management commitment, or lack thereof, as one of the biggest surprises he encountered throughout his 16 years in CRM:

> I've been surprised by how firms have understaffed and underestimated the effort it's going to take [to implement CRM]. And I want to accentuate effort. Not at the level of particular staffing decisions. A lot of time firms say "We've got the resources. We've got the IT team aligned. We've got a CRM Admin. We've even hired an offshore data steward group to clean data." I mean the effort from a leadership perspective and commitment to actually be involved in the project.[15]

A 2009 study peeled back a layer of the impact of top management, noting that it did not simply set the direction for initiatives, but it was also important that management "clearly understand the role of IT technologies as tools to enhance the overall strategic direction of the whole organization."[14] To that end, one reason management support might be either lacking or ineffective is the prevalence of technology illiteracy. The theme of technology literacy presents itself over and over throughout the CRM literature. In a 2012 article by Dong examining IT governance (discussed in greater detail later in this book), the author found in his examination of a particular firm that since the top management team in his firm didn't have technical expertise, "they [were] not aware of the potential benefits of CRM and [made] no efforts toward advocating CRM."[16] The study found that while CIOs and IT managers are typically strong advocates, their scope and reach in influencing the business are often limited, but can be expanded via effective governance and by effectively positioning the Technology Division, a topic we will unpack in a subsequent chapter. In their 2013 study, Law, Ennew, and Mitussis underscored not simply the importance of expertise and advocacy, but they also noted that in order "to have a successful implementation, management must understand both industry best practices and the adaptive capacity of their own organizations."[17] Management transparency is also important. In 2005, Avlonitis and Panagopoulos found that clarification of how "the system can be used for performing sales tasks and of what the management expects from its use, can boost [salesperson] performance."[18]

Company Size

In a study of technology innovation—and CRM is an example of such innovation—Ko, Kim, Kim, and Woo found that "large companies tend to adopt innovations more easily than small ones because they have good risk management abilities, abundant available resources, and strong infrastructures."[19] While CRM may ultimately have greater odds of success in a large company, it is most certainly not the case that large companies necessarily meet any of the three criteria noted above. Small firms operating in a less complicated environment may well have superior infrastructure to larger firms who have not prioritized infrastructure initiatives. The literature is mixed, however, regarding organizational size and CRM success correlation. In their examination of both organization size and organization age, Law, Ennew, and Mitussis found "no significant association between these two constructs and the adoption of CRM."[17]

CRM Maturity

If your firm is just dipping its toes in the ocean of CRM, this factor is not applicable and—even for firms with long-standing CRM initiatives—this is neither a necessary nor a sufficient condition to achieve CRM success. At least one study on enterprise knowledge management by Garrido-Moreno and Padilla-Melendez found, however, that "as firms use CRM, they experience an organizational learning that helps them to use the strategy more efficiently, and so the results of the strategy improve."[20] As we will note throughout this book, simply having played in the CRM space for a while has the significant potential to result in negative outcomes, especially if employees are dissatisfied with the quality of the system. This reality is further underscored by practitioners' observations that much of the CRM work they perform is in the context of CRM reimplementation. As a result, we might say that CRM maturity has the potential to be a positive indicator, but not in scenarios where poor implementations had occurred in the past.

Collaboration

A number of studies have shown the importance of teamwork and collaboration in the context of CRM. In one study, Ko, Kim, Kim, and Woo "examined levels of collaboration between marketing and IT teams and discovered that such collaboration was critical to the success of a CRM strategy."[19] Gaining value in the form of process efficiency, improved customer relationships, and firm performance requires collaboration beyond simply marketing and IT, but across all business areas. To that end, a successful company will be structured in a way that fosters cross-functional communication and collaboration. We will explore mechanisms to achieve these results in our discussion of employee alignment.

As we discussed briefly earlier in this book, the trend in CRM literature continually moves away from the specifics of technology, diminishing the focus on technical factors as drivers of success. Much literature implores us to consider everything from a process perspective first and a technical perspective second. A 2011 analysis of CRM in the retail banking industry by Saxena and Khandelwal reminds us that "CRM should not be taken as a tool for granting success; it should be implemented as part of a philosophy...."[21] That philosophy, however, manifests itself—or aims to—via very specific technical attributes. Once these philosophies are translated into technical attributes, an interesting phenomenon occurs: the technical attributes of a CRM system can—in a circular fashion—influence CRM strategy.

The concept being described above is a facet of business→IT alignment: the harmony of business strategy and processes with underlying IT systems. While this relationship can be—and often is—taken as one-way and linear, Sen and Sinha's 2011 study confirms the circular structure referenced above, noting that "IT alignment in CRM switches its anchors as it evolves. That is, in some stages, it anchors on business strategy, and in others it anchors on IT strategy."[22]

This is one of the most important observations we have made so far. One reason that many firms have focused primarily on business strategy is the advent of packaged CRM solutions. Many of these systems—especially hosted systems—provide little opportunity for enhancement or technical creativity, which has led companies to conclude that it must be the business strategy that is at fault, rather than the quality of the software and the adoption of that software by the user community.

The importance of technical factors in the success of CRM is underscored by another study on ERP systems—in many ways analogous to CRM systems—which found "a significant, positive relationship between ERP system quality and the individual impact in the context of ERP systems...."[2] In this context, the notion of individual impact refers to a given user's ability to effectively perform his business functions. These studies confirm the importance of technology in enabling business success. In 2005, Roh, Ahn, and Han found in their study that "many managers are now appreciating the wider strategic implications of developing a robust and responsive IT infrastructure...."[1] There is still much work to be done in this area, and technologists should bring forward the sort of concrete evidence referenced in the above studies in their efforts to demonstrate their division's posture toward driving business outcomes. We will discuss mechanisms to sell technology to the business in another chapter.

Readiness Methodology

While exploring the details of the methodology used to identify organizational readiness is largely outside the scope of this text, firms can benefit from pursuing initiatives to gain clarity on their readiness to implement CRM. It may not be that a specific methodology is needed to succeed, but the very act of introspection might yield significant insights that can improve firms' ability to achieve their goals. In his 2006 study, Chalmeta outlined what he calls the CRM-Iris methodology, which is comprised of the following:

1. Project management and prerequisites
2. Definition of the company's organizational framework
3. Definition of a customer strategy
4. Designing a customer relationship assessment system
5. Process map
6. Human resources [organization] and management
7. Construction of the information system
8. Implementation
9. Monitoring[7]

These points can serve as a foundation for firms as they prepare for CRM implementation. Uncovering blind spots ahead of the implementation could lead to significant savings in cost or professional quality of life. Firms will benefit from this type of introspection and planning in the context of all potential innovations.

Chapter Summary

Having surveyed a substantial portion of CRM literature, we have explored various risk factors and potential barriers to entry. The consensus is clear that lack of top management support is the most common reason for CRM failure. The remaining factors identified during this chapter are not listed in a particular order, but rather represent a high-level sampling of the items that have plagued folks during their CRM implementations. The following table represents a brief summary of the key risk items:

CONCEPT	EXPLANATION AND COMMENTARY
Lack of management support	Including lack of technical acumen in scenarios where management is supportive conceptually but has no technology context.
Cultural failures	These are vast and primarily include the lack of definition and implementation of a customer-centric culture prior to CRM deployment.
Data quality concerns	Could result from data conversion from prior system, but more likely the result of poor system design or lack of unified data entry processes.
Change management	Broadly includes lack of user education, lack of user solicitation (related to final point below), and issues with prior system migration (if applicable).
Neglecting strategy and process for technology	We posit that technology is responsible for more problems than many folks would like to admit, but the general consensus is that many firms have looked to technology as the answer at the expense of reviewing processes and strategy.
Insufficient user consultation	Users who have not been involved in the requirements, design, testing, and deployment of the CRM are significantly more likely to resist adoption.

References

1. Roh, T. H., Ahn, C. K., & Han, I. (2005). The priority factor model for customer relationship management system success. *Expert Systems with Applications 28*, 641–654.
2. Ifinedo, P. (2011). Examining the influences of external expertise and in-house computer/IT knowledge on ERP system success. *The Journal of Systems and Software 84*, 2065–2078.
3. Iriana, R., Buttle, F., & Ang, L. (2013). Does organisational culture influence CRM's financial outcomes. *Journal of Marketing Management 29(3–4)*, 467–493.
4. Ahearne, M., Hughes, D. E., & Schillewaert, N. (2007). Why sales reps should welcome information technology: Measuring the impact of CRM-based IT on sales effectiveness. *Internal Journal of Research in Marketing 24*, 336–349.
5. Anonymous. (2016, January 12–13). Making CRM successful—CRM practitioner interview (S. J. Kinnett, Interviewer).
6. Park, J. E., Kim, J., Dubinsky, A. J., & Lee, H. (2010). How does sales force automation influence relationship quality and performance? The

mediating roles of learning and selling behaviors. *Industrial Marketing Management 39*, 1128–1138.

7. Chalmeta, R. (2006). Methodology for customer relationship management. *The Journal of Information Systems and Software 79*, 1015–1024.

8. Pullig, C., Maxham III, J. G., & Hair, J. F. (2002). Salesforce automation systems: An exploratory examination of organizational factors associated with effective implementation and salesforce productivity. *Journal of Business Research 55*, 401–415.

9. Keramati, A., Nazari-Shirkouhi, S., Moshki, H., Afshari-Mofrad, M., & Maleki-Berneti, E. (2013). A novel methodology for evaluating the risk of CRM projects in fuzzy environment. *Neural Computing and Applications 23(Suppl. 1)*, 29–53.

10. Newell, F. (2003). *Why CRM Doesn't Work: How to Win by Letting Customers Manage the Relationship*. Princeton, NJ: Bloomberg Press.

11. Ang, L., & Buttle, F. (2006). CRM software applications and business performance. *Database of Marketing & Customer Strategy Management 14*, 4–16.

12. Battor, M., & Battor, M. (2010, August). The impact of customer relationship management capability on innovation and performance advantages: Testing a mediated model. *Journal of Marketing Management 26(9–10)*, 842–857.

13. Chung, Y. C., Hsu, Y. W., Tsai, S. C., Huang, H. L., & Tsai, C. H. (2012). The correlation between business strategy, information technology, organisational culture, implementation of CRM, and business performance in a high-tech industry. *South African Journal of Industrial Engineering 23*, 1–15.

14. Elmuti, D., Jia, H., & Gray, D. (2009, February). Customer relationship management strategic application and organizational effectiveness: An empirical investigation. *Journal of Strategic Marketing 17(1)*, 75–96.

15. Schneider, B., & Kippley, T. (2016, February 18). CRM practitioners—Rightpoint (S. J. Kinnett, Interviewer).

16. Dong, S. (2012). Decision execution mechanisms of IT governance: The CRM case. *International Journal of Information Management 32*, 147–157.

17. Law, A. K., Ennew, C. T., & Mitussis, D. (2013). Adoption of customer relationship management in the service sector and its impact on performance. *Journal of Relationship Marketing 12*, 301–330.

18. Avlonitis, G. J., & Panagopoulos, N. G. (2005). Antecedents and consequences of CRM technology acceptance in the sales force. *Industrial Marketing Management 34*, 355–368.

19. Ko, E., Kim, S. H., Kim, M., & Woo, J. Y. (2008). Organizational characteristics and the CRM adoption process. *Journal of Business Research, 61*, 65–74.

20. Garrido-Moreno, A., & Padilla-Melendez, A. (2011). Analyzing the impact of knowledge management on CRM success: The mediating effects of organizational factors. *International Journal of Information Management 31*, 437–444.

21. Saxena, R. P., & Khandelwal, P. K. (2011). Exploring customer perception and behavior towards CRM practices in banking sector: An empirical analysis. *The International Journal of Interdisciplinary Social Sciences 5(9)*, 375–391.

22. Sen, A., & Sinha, A. P. (2011). IT alignment strategies for customer relationship management. *Decision Support Systems 51*, 609–619.

4
UNDERSTANDING CRM
ADOPTION

A number of measures have been proposed to evaluate the success of customer relationship management (CRM) initiatives. As we will explore elsewhere, some firms may lean too far toward revenue as the primary measure of success when they may actually be realizing other intermediate gains such as operational efficiencies. Adoption of the system by its user base is widely considered as a precondition for realizing other successes from CRM, and as a result, adoption is the primary goal for which organizations should drive in order to realize subsequent benefits. In this chapter, we will explore exactly what adoption is and build a strategic foundation from which to draw in subsequent chapters.

What Is Adoption?

Before exploring specific constructs through which adoption can be measured, predicted, and driven, we pause to review research that seeks to provide insight into the most foundational of questions: what exactly is adoption? In an etymological study conducted in 2007, Schwarz and Chin used Borsodi's principles for their evaluation. Using this approach, the authors derived five dimensions:

- Receive
- Grasp
- Assess
- Be given
- Submit

These dimensions do not occur in isolation but rather are relative to a process component. In other words, as noted by Schwarz and Chin in 2007, "an individual engages in a series of psychological actions that can (or cannot) increase in frequency over time and result in a state of being, and eventually, automaticity."[1] We should highlight again that these cognitive paradigms do not occur in isolation but rather are interweaved with "contextual factors on the IS acceptance process."[1] We will explore models of the information system (IS) acceptance process that will ultimately allow us to juxtapose the psychological insights discussed above with existing models of technology acceptance to arrive at a complete picture of how adoption works and how we can leverage this understanding to improve adoption in our own firms.

This investigation paves the way for further research aimed at expanding our understanding of the five etymological dimensions already identified. This study will allow others to explore other facets of psychological acceptance, "including the extent to which an individual questions the IT, has a mental model of the IT, examines the desirability of the IT, has a willingness to psychologically adapt, and can surrender to the intentionality of the IT."[1] In their concluding remarks, Schwarz and Chin postulate whether all of the dimensions apply or become equally relevant throughout the totality of information technology (IT) use or whether instead they may be of interest during the initial adoption process. The dimensions at present do not have defined temporal relationships between one another (does one dimension follow from another?). The authors also ask researchers in the future to explore the impact of the dimensions on optimal use, efficiency, or driving innovative (sometimes referred to as extended or postadoptive) use of technology.

Adoption's Theoretical Frameworks and Foundations

Central to our understanding of antecedents of CRM adoption will be the mechanisms through which we measure adoption. Having now gained an understanding of what components comprise adoption, we can now turn to the variables that influence adoption. The theoretical underpinnings of technology acceptance have been explored extensively over the past two decades. The better our tools for evaluation, the better our ability to identify sticking points inhibiting CRM adoption and remove those barriers so that successful adoption can take place. A recurring theme upon which we will adhere is the coupling of academic research with processional experience. Understanding both types of information is important, and practitioners should understand that—however theoretical some of these concepts may seem—they are based on careful study and can be very informative along our path to success.

The Technology Acceptance Model

In 1986, Fred Davis published an essay which forever transformed the IS landscape. In the essay, *Perceived Usefulness, Perceived Ease of Use, and User Acceptance of Information Technology*, he introduced the idea of a model to predict technology acceptance via evaluation of two variables: perceived ease of use (PEOU) and perceived usefulness (PU). These independent variables were theorized to predict two dependent variables: behavioral intention (BI) and behavior (B). This framework of interrelated variables became known as technology acceptance model (TAM). The model received wide acclaim. Lee, Kozar, and Larsen noted that it received 424 citations in professional journals by the year 2000 and 698 citations by 2003.

Put simply, TAM "suggests that people who intend to use a particular technology end up using this technology to a larger extent than those who do not, and that people who find a technology useful and easy to use will intend to use it."[2] The fields of information sciences and management of IS were so transformed by TAM that authors Lee, Kozar, and Larsen unabashedly praise TAM as the most influential and commonly employed theory for describing an individual's acceptance of information systems.[3]

TAM's Major Constructs

Authors Lee, Kozar, and Larsen, through their research, provided additional clarity on the relationships between the TAM variables. They noted that "PU is used as both a dependent and independent variable since it is predicted by PEOU, and predicts BI and B at the same time."[3] In other words, a user's PEOU of a particular technology—in our case, our new CRM system—influences their thoughts on the usefulness of the technology, regardless of the objective realities of usefulness. This finding will be critical throughout much of our subsequent discussions throughout the remainder of this book. While we will shortly see that TAM has been expanded to encompass even more theories, the core reliability of TAM remains relevant and uncompromised.

Further research into the relationships between the TAM variables found that even though increasing PEOU increased perceptions of usefulness, if the system was not objectively useful, PEOU was not enough in and of itself to drive behavior. In other words, PEOU cannot compensate for uselessness. In summary, when the easy interfaces and smooth design draw users toward a cognitive paradigm where they are open to the system *also* being useful and not just easy to use, it is that assessment of actual usefulness which will drive adoption.

Initiation and Reception

TAM has been commended as a seminal research insight that ultimately offered a substantial contribution to the IS field. It sets itself apart—in another way—because such formal theories are rare. Scholars were able to leverage TAM to conduct their own studies. Finally finding themselves grounded in a sound theoretical framework, IS researchers had an abundance of options upon which to build future studies. Such evolution was critical, with one study noting that "growing and refining the theoretical foundation with tested measurement instruments will serve to legitimize the [Information Sciences] field in the eyes of other business disciplines."[3] Relevant to the CRM space, TAM has notably served as a foundational, theoretical framework for marketing studies.

Critique

Despite the lavish praise of the academic community, as we noted above, TAM received criticism early for its focus on PEOU as having a slightly more direct contribution to BI and B, rather than influencing PU more directly. Beyond simply its theoretical underpinnings, TAM—when translated into plain business speak—created awkward scenarios. As Lee, Kozar, and Larsen—big fans of TAM—noted earlier, "TAM's simplicity makes it difficult to put into practice. Practitioners may not be well served by TAM."

> imagine talking to a manager and saying that to be adopted technology must be useful and easy to use. I imagine the reaction would be "Duh!" The more important questions are what makes technology useful and easy to use.
>
> **Alan Dennis.**[3]

It is eliminating that "duh factor," which scholars have sought to address in the subsequent literature both by extending TAM and by providing supplementary theories and contextual, external variables. Many of the variables would be typical for any studies of this nature including the use of questionnaire-based studies, conducting many studies on students in academic environments rather than actual business technology practitioners, drawing conclusions from point-in-time evaluation rather than measures over time, and others. All of these factors—coupled with the excitement surrounding TAM's potential—led to voluminous research that followed TAM's debut and paved the way for subsequent and related constructs including TAM2 and the unified theory of the acceptance and use of technology (UTAUT), which extended the primary TAM with additional context and contributions of mediating factors.

In a 2003 study, Venkatesh, Morris et al. laid the foundation of UTAUT,[4] which is a unified and extended model for technology acceptance. This new model linked TAM to the theory of rational action (TRA), the motivational model, the theory of planned behavior (TPB) model of personal computer (PC) utilization, innovation diffusion theory, and social cognitive theory. The unification of so many models directly addressed the core criticism of TAM, which was that it was too simple and arguably obvious when applied to real enterprise technology adoption scenarios. The UTAUT encompasses four major dimensions: performance expectancy, effort expectancy, social expectancy, and facilitating expectancy.

Despite this evolution in theory, many researchers continued to use the seminal TAM as basis for their additional evaluations. In a 2013 study, Svendsen et al. found that the TAM may be limited in its ability to predict adoption, particularly as the model pertains to the *behavioral intent* (*BI*) variable. In the study, they sought to clarify the role of user personality on behavioral intent. The authors argue that user personality impacts behavioral intent in ways that TAM constructs have not accounted for. As a result, researchers and practitioners looking to leverage TAM/UTAUT constructs "need to be concerned with the personality of the research participants."[2]

This insight underscores our deep examination of salespeople as users having distinct personalities and reminding us that focusing on a specific population of homogeneous users is one of the more effective ways to conduct these sorts of analyses. The additional constructs provided by the UTAUT include both individuals' cognitive orientation toward technology and social variables. This was a necessary extension of TAM that allowed it to become exponentially more relevant to practitioners. We will find these social variables of great importance throughout much of our discussion on topics ranging from training behaviors to gamification and incentive programs.

Peer Pressure and Subjective Norm

One element of someone's personality that has been shown to be relevant to CRM adoption is his or her orientation toward peer pressure. Peer pressure (or group pressure) is known within the literature and adoption models as *subjective norm*, defined as "a person's perception that most people who are important to him think he should or should not perform the behavior in question."[5] For those with susceptible personalities, peer pressure is as useful as it was in high school when it comes to CRM adoption. The analogy is incomplete, however, in that peer pressure does not necessarily carry a negative connotation. Competitions and incentives—gamification—are also grounded in peer-pressure, subjective norm. To the latter, when incentives are implemented such that each user must make a significant contribution for the team to win overall, the user will be more likely to embrace the technology. A 2013 study confirmed this, noting that "when a salesperson is not motivated to use SFA technologies for individualistic reasons, he or she will be motivated and pressured by other salespeople to use the technology because of the team-based incentive."[6]

In addition to using group incentives to harness the power of peer pressure, interactions with colleagues about CRM can also improve individual expectations. To that end, "when salespeople can see the positive outcomes of IT acceptance among their colleagues, they may value these tools more highly and be willing to invest the effort necessary to learn to use them and regularly incorporate them into their daily activities."[7] The importance of top management support appeared again in an empirical study conducted in 2011 by Pai and Tu, who found that CRM advocacy driven by someone with power and authority in an organization has a strong correlation to CRM usage by employees. We knew that top management support was critical for CRM success, and this is one way in which such support manifests in real terms and is underscored by the literature.

Utilizing peer pressure can be difficult in models where sales reps are not geographically centralized, such as pharmaceutical sales reps. These folks are used to operating on their own, and sales management must take special care not to reinforce this structural reality with its incentive structure. One examination of the existing landscape concluded that "although collectivistic goals and tasks are valued and often promoted by organizations, few attempts are made to manifest them through compensation at the field sales level, especially in traditionally individualistically oriented countries"[6] such as the United States. These data suggest that ample opportunities exist for firms to implement collective incentives. We will explore a particular collection of incentives collectively referred to as gamification, which is emerging with significant popularity in the CRM space. Leaderboards and other in-system rewards or recognition mechanisms could be used even in geographically dispersed sales models.

Tim Kippley of Rightpoint Consulting provided additional insight into the particulars of incentives and adoption strategies. He believes that incentives are important and can range along the spectrums of both carrot→stick and tactical→strategic. To the tactical side, he notes that the advent of gamification tools has allowed organizations to easily "create badges or awards or rewards for, as an example, who merged the most contacts. You'd be surprised for a 10 dollar Starbucks card what people will do. Or even for competition's sake, people will want the recognition and be able to say: 'hey I'm the data quality rock star of the week.'"[8]

Kippley also noted that salespeople, in particular, tend to have a natural competitiveness that can be harnessed to increase CRM adoption. The potential for transparency in CRM—a potential point of salesperson resistance—can fire up salespeople when properly implemented. The classic Leaderboard, showing who has the most "points," is effective when coupled with appropriate rewards. Organizations can also increase adoption by designing their business processes in a way that necessitates system usage. For professional services firms, this could be as simple as requiring opportunities to be input into the system or they will be viewed as if they did not happen. Kippley has found this to be another area where top management support and leadership are necessary to set and enforce expectations. Clayton Wolf, a consultant with Kenway Consulting, extended a specific process→technology alignment decision that forced CRM adoption: the implementation of customer billing within the CRM system. "Because the CRM was utilized for billing, it would be essentially impossible to proceed through the sales cycle without the entry. If opportunity details went in at the last minute, hands got slapped."[9] A combination of process decisions, formal incentives, and clear expectations will likely be effective during the adoption process.

Individual Innovativeness and TAM Variables

Further extending our discussion of TAM contextual variables explored in UTAUT, we can now turn to personal or individual innovativeness. As noted above, UTAUT was informed by Innovation Diffusion Theory. This theory defines a collection of characteristics called innovation characteristics, which "can be determined by three categories of factors: (i) features of the technology, (ii) attributes of the person, and (iii) situational factors."[10] These definitions are useful to firms as they look to build a more innovative culture. In the context of technology adoption, these characteristics may be beneficial as they allow us to draw a connection between individual innovativeness and BI.

Further research into means to uncover specific characteristics and how to evaluate those characteristics in an interview context would be a logical next step, though it is outside the scope of this text. As further evidence that hiring individuals with an innovation orientation (and cultivating individual innovativeness within existing employees) is useful, Yi et al. in their 2006 study found that "individual innovativeness was a *direct determinant* of user perceptions of usefulness, ease of use, and compatibility."[10] Translating all this theory to practice, the study reminds us that CRM success is influenced by the users themselves and in particular, users' innovation orientation or individual innovativeness. This realization is paramount in that it provides clear evidence that even the most effectively engineered CRM initiatives are still subject to personnel considerations. This suggests firms should look for individual innovativeness during the hiring process and for opportunities to increase this characteristic among existing employees. Pursuing employee alignment initiatives (discussed in the next chapter) will be useful in ensuring collective terminology and cross-functional understanding.

Chapter Summary

In this chapter, we have explored adoption's theoretical frameworks. We began with TAM and explored subsequent evolutions of this model such as the UTAUT. We have discussed details of specific adoption variables such as individual innovativeness, personalities, and peer pressure. Understanding these frameworks and contextual variables will serve as foundations as we evaluate strategies to drive adoption during the CRM implementation process in subsequent chapters.

Despite our explorations of TAM extensions, we will continue to leverage TAM throughout the remainder of the book. While the criticisms are not invalid, TAM has not been shown to be inaccurate. We posit that mastering fundamentals is key to CRM success, and TAM is both simple and represents the fundamentals of adoption theory. Where the research lends itself to evaluating extensions to TAM in the context of our discussions, we will include that research and its implications to our adoption approach. What we have explored in our discussion and will continue to explore is the literature on mitigating and contextual factors that could diminish or extend the influence of TAM in specific circumstances.

We also have examined gamification and incentives as mechanisms to improve adoption, understanding that these approaches leverage core psychological paradigms of particular presence in salespeople. Gamification is also an important component of ongoing CRM management, discussed in Part 3, especially in the context of ongoing and future initiatives and keeping users engaged after deployment. But first, in the next chapter, we will explore business→IT alignment: an important construct which has vast implications on CRM success.

References

1. Schwarz, A., & Chin, W. (2007, April). Looking forward: Toward an understanding of the nature and definition of IT acceptance. *Journal of the Association for Information Systems 8(4)*, 230–243.
2. Svendsen, G. B., Johnsen, J.-A. K., Almas-Sorensen, L., & Vitterso, J. (2013). Personality and technology acceptance: The influence of personality factors on the core constructs of the technology acceptance model. *Behaviour & Information Technology 32(4)*, 323–334.
3. Lee, Y., Kozar, K. A., & Larsen, K. R. (2003). The technology acceptance model: Past, present, and future. *Communications of the Association for Information Systems, 12(50)*, 752–780.
4. Venkatesh, V., Morris, M. G., Davis, G. B., and Davis, F. D. (2003). User acceptance of information technology: Toward a unified view. *MIS Quarterly 27(3)* 425–478
5. Venkatesh, V., & Davis, F. D. (2000). A theoretical extension of the technology acceptance model: Four longitudinal field studies. *Management Science 46(2)*, 186–204.
6. Baker, D. S., & Delpechitre, D. (2013). Collectivistic and individualistic performance expectancy in the utilization of sales automation technology in an international field sales setting. *Journal of Personal Selling & Sales Management 33(3)*, 277–288.
7. Ahearne, M., Hughes, D. E., & Schillewaert, N. (2007). Why sales reps should welcome information technology: Measuring the impact of CRM-based IT on sales effectiveness. *Internal Journal of Reasearch in Marketing 24(4)*, 336–349.
8. Kippley, T., & Schneider, B. (2016, February 18). CRM practitioners—Rightpoint (S. J. Kinnett, Interviewer).
9. Wolff, Clayton. (2016). Making CRM sucecssful—CRM practitioner interview. (S. J. Kinnett, Interviewer).
10. Yi, M. Y., Fiedler, K. D., & Park, J. S. (2006, August). Understanding the role of individual innovativeness in the acceptance of IT-based innovations: Comparative analyses of models and measures. *Decision Sciences 337(3)*, 393–426.

5

BUSINESS–IT ALIGNMENT

In the previous chapter, we briefly touched upon the importance of alignment between business units and the Technology Division. While achieving this alignment is paramount for all firms to relationship value from their technology initiatives, we will see that customer relations management (CRM)—as a key innovation—benefits or suffers from the sophistication of a firm's alignment. The extant literature has proposed several definitions of business→information technology (IT) alignment. Wong, Ngan, Chan, and Chong described in their study alignment as "the appropriate application of information technologies in supporting a company's strategies, goals and needs."[1] Taking this notion to a more granular level, Burn and Szeto characterized alignment as an understanding that "business success depends on the linkage of business strategy, IT strategy, organizational infrastructure and processes, and IT infrastructure and processes."[2] But perhaps the best definition we found in the surveyed literature was presented by Jorfi and Jorfi, who described alignment as "the degree that business mission, objectives and plans support and, at the same time, are supported by information technology mission, objectives and plans."[3] This definition gets at the circular nature of business strategy and IT strategy we saw in Chapter 2; that is, business strategy influences technology strategy which, in turn, shapes business strategy. If a firm views the Technology function diminutively and embraces only the one-way approach, it may miss out on the ways in which technology can help shape business strategy.

In a global survey conducted in 2012, Luftman, Zadeh, Derksen, Santana, Rigoni, and Huang reported that alignment continues to be a major challenge, noting "in all of the geographies, IT and business alignment ranks in the top 10 management concerns; ranking 1st in the US and Europe, 2nd in Latin America, and 6th in Asia."[4] One of the factors underlying the necessity of IT and business alignment is to help technology prove the business value of IT. As we will see in the next chapter, the Technology Division has much to consider as it looks to position itself for success, and pursuing alignment initiatives is paramount to the division's ability to shine.

In practical terms, we achieve alignment when "goals, activities and processes of a business organization are in harmony with the information systems supporting them."[5] Achieving alignment allows firms to realize a number of benefits including competitive advantage, increased return on IT investment, and improved project lifecycles resulting from stronger communication between business units and IT. When it comes to CRM alignment in particular, we are referring to an alignment of the sales and marketing verticals to the CRM technology system and corresponding CRM strategy. In Chapter 1, we highlighted the unique nature of CRM among other innovations. While achieving alignment between the Technology Division and every business unit is important, a 2012 study by Aversano, Grasso, and Tortorella found that, in particular, the alignment of Technology with the marketing function resulted in improvements to both the marketing function and the firm's overall success.

Core Alignment Components

In 2011, Jorfi and Jorfi proposed three key direct contributors to IT alignment: IT flexibility, IT capability, and communications effectiveness. These three components, they posit, are mediated by effective information systems planning. Figure 5.1 outlines this proposed relationship.

IT flexibility and communications effectiveness are each the summation of three components. The first, IT flexibility, is the degree to which the Technology function responds effectively to change and is facilitated by achievements in software modularity, hardware compatibility, and network connectivity. It is important to note that flexibility refers to very specific technical components, distinguishing it from IT capability, which refers to IT employee skill level and human capital management capability. The final core component is communication effectiveness: the measure of how a sender's thoughts are transcribed to words and subsequently understood by a receiver. In this context, effectiveness is the result of skill, motivation, and knowledge; that

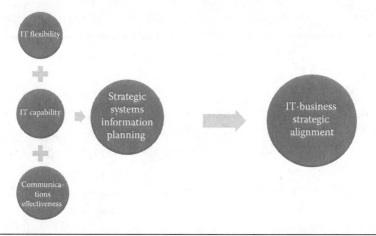

Figure 5.1 Components of strategic alignment.

is, one must have the verbal and written communication skills to be able to convey his or her ideas, he or she must be motivated to put in the effort to do so, and finally he or she must know what he or she is talking about. We will see these themes reflected in our upcoming discussion of employee alignment.

The degree to which IT flexibility, IT capability, and effective communication can influence alignment is mediated by the strategic planning surrounding information systems—also known as Strategic Information Systems Planning. Successful planning in this regard is the result of effective "problem identification, environmental scanning, and ability to embrace change, and an ability to use these capabilities for aligning IT with business strategy."[3] One of the most significant takeaways resulting from this structure is that the systems themselves and the effective planning of system development stand as a gatekeeper of sorts between other contributing components and successful alignment. The systems have to be there, they have to be well thought-out, and they have to work.

Employee Alignment

Consistent with our core goal of understanding the human component as it relates to the successful strategy, implementation, and management of CRM systems, we will now examine the role of what can be called *employee alignment*, which serves as a precursor to the achievement of business–IT alignment. The specific components of employee alignment that are considered to be relevant to achieving business–IT alignment are "perceived employee trust, perceived communications on business–IT strategies to employees, perceived employee commitment to business–IT strategy, and perceived employee knowledge."[1]

Think of employee alignment as the channel through which specific systems, such as CRM, can become aligned with business processes. Employee alignment occurs when employees demonstrate commitment, which flows through to business–IT alignment via the mediating channels of trust and communication, with organizational knowledge being a necessary precursor to communication. Employee alignment pertains to employees in both business and technology verticals. Misalignment of employees with each other is characterized by lack of harmony in objectives and culture and likely a mutual ignorance of each other's job functions or organizational knowledge. Figure 5.2 outlines the relationship between these employee alignment components.

Achieving employee alignment between technology personnel and salespeople is important to achieving CRM success. Salespeople, as we have begun to see and will continue to explore in greater depth, are often severely lacking in technical acumen. Technologists are often outsourced or otherwise geographically distant, which may prevent them from—at least until they have realized significant tenure working with a particular business unit—gaining sufficient "business speak" to interface successfully. This results in a scenario where we find ourselves drawing from different vocabularies. Lack of common knowledge and language gives rise to the mutual ignorance referenced

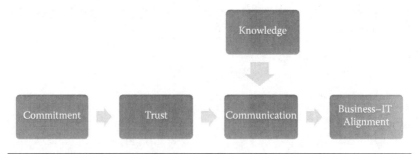

Figure 5.2 Employee alignment diagram.

above which all too often clouds employee interactions. The extant literature calls out salespeople once again, noting that alignment is, for the sales organization, "one of the highest hurdles to clear"[6] both because salespeople have often operated as lone wolves and have their own methodology, and because, in the absence of clearly defined benefits, salespeople are not interested in diverting time away from clients to learn a new toy. The successful alignment of business objectives and corresponding IT implementations requires first that employees achieve alignment with each other. We will now explore in detail the specific components of employee alignment: communication, trust, and knowledge.

Communication

Communication—often cited as a critical problem in business, politics, life, and love—is defined in the context of business–IT alignment as "the process of exchanging information, knowledge and ideas among the IT and business professionals, in ensuring that the business and IT sides have mutual understanding of the business and IT environments, and of the organization's strategies."[1] In our diagram, communication is the final gatekeeper to achieving alignment. Communication sits as an intermediary between knowledge and trust.

Our model shows that the relationship between communication and commitment is mediated by trust—underscoring that even the best communication will not be received in the absence of trust, thereby almost guaranteeing that commitment cannot be achieved. Communication is, however, the direct bridge from knowledge to business–IT alignment. As it pertains to the employee component, communication remains quintessential for business–IT alignment. Our ultimate goal is to connect the dots between employee commitment and business–IT alignment, understanding that the role of knowledge feeds directly into communication.

Trust

While communication is the core concept that brings together knowledge and employee commitment, it is trust which can at times be the most elusive goal to achieve. We can define trust in this context as a moment when, "in the pursuit of a mutually beneficial outcome or a common goal, an employee voluntarily becomes vulnerable to another."[1] The myriad ways to foster employee trust are largely outside the scope of this text, but one example of a scenario that can inspire trust is a shared goal. When top management, for example, communicates a clear and actionable goal that requires folks to work together, trust will come more easily.

Knowledge

Knowledge is obviously a very broad term and could span from technical literacy—a necessary but not sufficient component to achieving CRM success—to business process knowledge to a firm's business principles and basic procedures. Collectively, we might call this organizational *common knowledge*. Common knowledge includes common vocabulary. The larger the organization, the more likely that the body of common knowledge may be too great to be transmitted via organic training or employee onboarding. Instead, common knowledge is acquired only through the natural accumulation of working within a particular functional area. Organizational knowledge includes values, insights, experience, and contextual information, and it is accumulated via organizational tenure. The proliferation of organizational common knowledge along with specific contextual knowledge has led to the need for methodologies and systems to manage this ever-increasing body of knowledge.

Consider the sheer volume of functional and technical knowledge necessary to thrive within the behemoths that are many current CRM systems. Knowledge management (KM) has emerged as a response to the challenge of managing and disseminating an increasing body of organizational knowledge. The importance of KM is underscored in the context of employee alignment. Wong, Ngan, Chan, and Chong reminded us in their 2012 study that a strong communication level can only be preserved in the presence of a reasonable amount of resources focused on knowledge acquisition and retention. CRM initiatives are sometimes viewed through the lens of KM initiatives. The type of information (knowledge) stored in CRM begins as *tacit knowledge*—knowledge understood by an individual but not translated into means that it can be consumed by others. A well-designed CRM system is built with a structure that is congruent with a person's cognitive structure as it pertains to the storage of tacit customer knowledge. The CRM system must be built in such a way that employees are guided through the entry of their tacit knowledge such that it becomes explicit and—as a consequence—available and useful to others. Tacit knowledge will become contextual knowledge and, when organized and disseminated effectively, may become organizational knowledge or common knowledge.

Perceptions on Organizational Alignment

In a 2000 study, Burn and Szeto examined the ways in which the alignment challenge manifests itself in real terms within organizations. They surveyed a number of business and IT professionals across multiple industry verticals. Among their findings was an observation that alignment varies by industry and by the level of reliance organizations have on the Technology Division. Other results revealed that business managers correctly identified top management support as a critical factor that may have been inhibiting alignment, whereas technology professionals cited that the lack of business units' understanding of IT's potential contributions resulted as the biggest hurdle in the alignment challenge. The answer is likely that both are significantly important and not mutually exclusive. Lobbying for top management support—especially in the CRM space—should be taken as an essential and ongoing requirement for achieving CRM success. It is also the case that improving technology literacy is a never-ending challenge which cannot be marginalized. We may think of literacy most directly as competence with the basic use of technology. On a more advanced level, however, it can be viewed as an understanding not only of what technology is, but also of what it can be. By educating employees on principles of technology and how they have been applied to the business, firms can—in effect—cultivate an environment conducive to technical innovation.

Chapter Summary

In this chapter, we learned that achieving alignment is critical to an organization's success and is ranked among the top of challenges organizations face. Our research has shown that alignment is not just perceived as being critical, but indeed has important implications on an organization's ability to succeed with CRM. Misalignment breeds misunderstood requirements, inferior expectations management capability, and reduced empathy among colleagues. We learned that oftentimes different parts of the organization may be mutually ignorant of one another's business functions and responsibilities. This makes it difficult for employees to relate to one another and understand challenges that may arise during CRM implementation.

We learned about three key direct contributors to IT alignment: IT flexibility, IT capability, and communications effectiveness. We examined the concept of employee alignment, which encompasses communication, trust, and knowledge. Successful employee alignment allows improved communication and collaboration, thereby increasing the likelihood of successful business→IT strategic alignment. Finally, we learned that business units and the Technology Division may be aware when they are out of alignment but each group has been shown to have varying perspectives on the causes or solutions to misalignments spanning ignorance of IT capability to lack of management support. As a result, we now know that continually enlisting top management support while driving initiatives to improve technical literacy will best position firms to overcome alignment challenges.

References

1. Wong, T., Ngan, S.-C., Chan, F. T., & Chong, A. Y.-L. (2012). A two-stage analysis of the influences of employee alignment on effecting business-IT alignment. *Decision Support Systems 53*, 490–498.
2. Burn, J. M., & Szeto, C. (2000). A comparison of the views of business and IT management on success factors for strategic alignment. *Information & Management 37*, 197–216.
3. Jorfi, S., & Jorfi, H. (2011). Strategic operations management: Investigating the factors impacting IT-business strategic alignment. *Procedia Social and Behavioral Sciences 24*, 1606–1614.
4. Luftman, J., Zadeh, S. H., Derksen, B., Santana, M., Rigoni, E. H., & Huang, Z. D. (2012). Key information technology and management issues 2011–2012: An international study. *Journal of Information Technology 27*, 198–212.

5. Aversano, L., Grasso, C., & Tortorella, M. (2012). A literature review of business/IT alignment strategies. *Procedia Technology 5*, 462–474.
6. Lager, M. (2007, July). The alignment: CRM capabilities and business processes enable technology to shine. *Customer Relationship Management*, pp. 46–49.

6

POSITIONING THE
TECHNOLOGY DIVISION

The move toward outsourcing and the trend of headcount and budget reductions for Technology Divisions have led the departments to be viewed as commodities in the worst sense of the word. In the long run, firms that have pushed this commoditization will find it backfiring. It may not be tomorrow, but a firm that under-funds, under-values, and under-resources its staff will find itself disempowered. The business–information technology (IT) dichotomy is a flawed structure to begin with, and it is only made worse by the marginalization of the chief information officer (CIO) function and the associated commoditization of the IT function. If you are a technologist reading this, we suspect you would agree.

This chapter explores mechanisms to aid in the effective positioning of the IT function in order to maximize customer relationship management (CRM) success. This concept encompasses the traditional notion of alignment. Several studies have suggested that the relationship management aspect of the Technology Division is behind many failures of IT to business alignment. As an example, a 2006 study concluded that, as it pertains to the IT function, the "lack of relationship management skills is one of the key inhibitors to maturity and success."[1] Although less visible in the literature, it is also the business's responsibility to partner with Technology on a leveled playing field so as to combat the dangerous dichotomy noted above. The progressive firm must realize the importance of IT as fundamental to the customer acquisition and retention process. As the general population becomes more and more comfortable using technology, reliance increases on IT both for customer-facing and for internal support systems.

We are advocating—we recognize—for a tectonic shift, and the reality is that the onus to bridge the gap will invariably fall to the

Technology Division. Most firms' client-facing business units are simply too taxed and facing their own resourcing constraints to focus on building relationships with Technology. One way firms can begin an organic process of bridging the two groups is by hiring folks with technical backgrounds into the business side of their organizations. Candidates with technical backgrounds in a liberal arts context often fit well into these business units and will be predisposed to be more empathetic toward the Technology Division, being more likely to understand complexities of software development, infrastructure maintenance, and project management.

The task before the Technology Division is to implement a CRM to help the success of the firm's CRM. In other words, the Technology function must implement a CRM strategy to help its firm's CRM strategy succeed. Technology's customers are the business units: sales, marketing, and service. As Technology begins to shape its CRM strategy, it will naturally arrive at the need to view itself as a market competitor with a collection of products and services that must be "sold" to its customers, the business units.

This is a fundamental shift for the Technology Division—in essence, going on offense. The Technology Division must change its focus from preventing problems to promoting solutions. In the 2013 book *Focus: Different Ways of Seeing the World for Success and Influence*, Drs. Tory E. Higgins and Heidi Grant define a *promotion focus* as a mental orientation concerned with "maximizing gains and avoiding missed opportunities."[2] When we strive to stand out and be recognized, to thrust ourselves before others without fear of scrutiny, we have embraced the promotion focus. The authors define the other side of this coin—the side on which the staggering majority of IT departments have now found themselves—as a *prevention focus*, which concerns itself with "minimizing losses to keep things working."[2]

Sometimes, IT organizations do seek to promote themselves, but they may be promoting the wrong things. An example we will reference often is the case of IT attempting to promote large, glamorous initiatives when the fundamentals are being ignored. In fact, when the ship is not secure, IT *should* be engaged in a prevention focus, which manifests itself "whenever we are trying to stay safe and secure, avoid mistakes, fulfill our duties and responsibilities, and be seen as reliable and steadfast."[2] Taken to its extreme, prevention focus is insecurity.

Promotion focus, on the other hand, when unchecked, leads to arrogance and delusion. The very structural orientation of many modern firms as it pertains to the juxtaposition of "the business" and the Technology Division facilitates a prevention-focused paradigm.

The challenge for the Technology Division is in breaking from the prevailing paradigm of prevention focus, which is especially challenging since it is embedded into the very fabric of organizational structure. Rightly or wrongly, Technology is often viewed as a cost center, and this orientation permeates the way IT addresses its tasks and challenges. Prevention-orientation is proper and appropriate in some contexts within the IT function—and all enterprise functions—but as it pertains to CRM, one study indicates, "companies that promote an atmosphere of innovation or risk taking, hence creating a climate for employees to act in the best interest of customers tend to fare better in their CRM outcomes."[3] We posit that a broader examination of your firm's orientation toward promotion or prevention will bring fruits outside of the CRM space alone. The underlying assumption made in the above is that the employees referenced are *able* to act in the best interest of customers. The precondition to this possibility is that the distance between employees—in this case, technologists—and customers is manageable, when the reality among many firms reveals this is not the case. A simple example, such as geographic silos, highlights the distance between technologists and customers—both its direct internal customers and also end clients.

One way that Technology can begin to change itself to a promotion paradigm is by adopting a *marketing lens*, which occurs when the Technology Division shapes its processes and relationships as if it were delivering a product, complete with all the classic marketing orientations surrounding product, price, promotion, and place, with the aim of meeting the needs of the customer. The word customer in this context refers to internal consumers of technology, such as the sales and marketing teams. Viewing the Technology function through this marketing lens admittedly opens up a number of potential risks. Hirschheim, Schwarz, and Todd noted in 2006 that adopting this marketing perspective effectively makes the Technology Division its own brand competing in the marketplace. As a result, the division must benchmark itself against competitors such as external vendors and other IT teams in its industry. This orientation directly positions the IT organization against external vendors. After all, under this model, a decision to select an external vendor is an indication that the business lacks any brand loyalty to its IT organization, right? Not necessarily, and jumping to this conclusion is a very real risk as we noted above in the example of firms that have urgent time-to-market concerns or other variables that may prevent a build decision from being the right one.

In its attempts to compete with the marketplace, via this "us vs. them" paradigm, the Technology Division will almost certainly be positioned to make overly aggressive estimates. While competition can be healthy, firms should remember that an underfunded IT organization will not be able to compete with a packaged software product—the development of which is one of the sole financial focuses of its creator. Thus, the comparison of internal IT to the market must be done with a very critical eye lest it unfairly paint apples to oranges comparisons. In other words, tossing IT up against others in the market and judging it solely on these comparisons is a recipe for misinformation, disillusionment, and ultimately divisional decline.

The basic act of making IT—and the value it adds—more visible to an organization can help to temper previously poor perceptions of the IT function. As folks become more and more aware of the challenging IT environment, they may become more sensitive to their colleagues' plight. Indeed, as with hiring technically sharp employees, raising awareness by any means leads to business units developing empathy with the Technology Division, a precursor to supporting the division. Clearly, the Technology organization needs to be very clear about its strengths and weaknesses, if it is to begin the process of going on offense and marketing itself. One way to facilitate this organizational learning is through an IT maturity model and customer definition exercise.

IT Maturity Model

In order for Technology to promote and position itself effectively to the business, it must first conduct a dispassionate self assessment. To that end, the mechanisms through which IT should market itself depend largely on how mature the Technology function is, which can be evaluated via a maturity model. Hirschheim,

Schwarz, and Todd concluded in their study conducted in 2006 that the Technology Division may evolve through three stages: competency, credibility, and commitment. My experience in the CRM space has found that far too often, the Technology Division is being pushed to deliver on higher-level initiatives when it has not been afforded opportunities to achieve competency, the first maturity level. A Technology group cannot graduate to the credibility level if it has not yet succeeded in demonstrating a "proven track record in the delivery of IT services, with 24/7 dependability."[1] Figure 6.1 shows the nature of the relationships between the components of the IT maturity model.

From a marketing perspective, a Technology group that identifies itself at Level 1 knows that it must increase stability and reliability of its systems and it also knows that it must drive home the improvements in this area before promoting additional services. An IT organization facing perceptions of failure at Level 1 will not be well positioned to begin pitching new products or services—despite the fact that it is also driven to do so, even when it is aware that such a progression is not yet warranted.

The second level, *credibility*, refers to "the ability of the IT organization to deliver the right systems to the right people, on time and within budget, in such a way as to satisfy a specific business need."[1] Obviously, this presupposes that whatever is already in place—whether or not it is the right system or aligned to the right users or satisfying the right

Figure 6.1   IT maturity model.

objectives—is at least reliable. IT consultants are usually presupposed to be competent or firms would not hire them, so consultants typically enter the game being assessed at the credibility level.

The top level of maturity is *commitment*, a level in which "IT serves as a strategic partner in the business, capable of solving strategic business problems."[1] One practical—if imperfect—way to determine whether or not your IT organization has reached this level is the way in which senior management brings technology projects to the table. If the question of evaluating a vendor does not come up, your organization likely has reached the commitment level. Another mechanism to determine commitment is how management responds to IT-driven proposals. As IT continues to align itself more and more effectively with the business, the business will—via a slow and organic process—come to take direction from IT.

If this sounds preposterous, it is because this top level of maturity is difficult to achieve and reaching it is predicated on nothing less than mastery of the prior two levels. If your CRM system is a mess, senior management will be unlikely to view the IT department as a strategic partner. What the Technology Division can do, however, is begin to "flip the script" by moving into promotion orientation and proposing initiatives to shore up those things that are broken. Over time, the business will see this paradigm shift, and as credibility surrounding basic functionality increases, the folks on the business side will be more likely to listen to the ideas IT has developed through its successful customer focus and alignment with the business.

As we turn our eyes toward our assessment of our own IT organization, we should remember that no organization will completely fit in one category. There may be some moments when systems go down, but that does not mean that the organization has always failed to deliver upon more strategic projects. The challenge arises when the Technology organization orients itself toward building more, newer, increasingly glamorous tools but leaves the support, enhancement, and infrastructure surrounding existing tools to inexperienced developers while simultaneously allocating those developers to additional initiatives. This overextension of junior resources ultimately results in poor technical support of existing systems.

It is just not as fun—for most—to dig into legacy software implementations, look for opportunities to tune database queries, and hunt for bugs within aged spaghetti code, as it is to whip open a fresh development environment and design something new and exciting. But this is precisely the trap that causes IT organizations to lose commitment and credibility. As support for keeping the lights on is either outsourced or de-prioritized (distinction without a difference), the Technology function will suddenly find angry users bellowing at the help desk and—worse—at senior management, who will quickly forget all of the flashy promises made in the name of enhancing the business and begin to question whether Technology can perform even its fundamental functions. The unfortunate reality is that 80% of Technology's credibility comes from 20% of the services they provide: specifically technical functionality, stability, and usability, which—incidentally—correspond to the design hierarchy of needs examined later in this book.

Internal Customer Definition

Just as a successful CRM initiative will identify and segment customers, so too can the IT organization segment its internal customers. These internal customers are transactional customers, relationship customers, and IT influencers. When we consider these designations, we should guard against over-architecting the way we view our organization. While the maturity model discussed previously is an important mechanism to allow IT to understand itself and shape its marketing strategy, customer definitions need not be an ongoing question to be evaluated at every turn: "Wait, before I answer this support request, is this a transactional or relationship customer?" All customers want the same things in the end: a robust, workable system supported by an intelligent and efficient staff.

A brief discussion of segmentation can be helpful in that it does help us shape our communication. Beginning with transactional customers, we should understand that their most important priority will be IT competency. In the CRM space, these are your frontline sales folks, customer service reps—anyone entering the system to perform specific, repeatable tasks on a periodic basis. They need the system to work, to be fast, and to be effective. These individuals are typically not involved in project discussions, but their input should always be part of any initiative. We will discuss the importance of transactional customers' presence in the postadoption section of this book.

The next level are relationship customers, who can be identified by their use and payment of multiple IT services. Relationship customers have longer-term relationships with the Technology Division and place a premium on the responsiveness of the IT function, their tacit assumption—or, sometimes, not so tacit—being that core reliability and durability have neither been sacrificed. These folks include the sales and marketing managers and some members of the steering committee. Some relationship customers are involved in requirements identification, and they are often—as in the case of the managers—taking aggregated feedback from their teams of transactional customers. Relationship customers will be asking for enhancements, even though they may not have direct knowledge of the system. Because they are in this intermediary role—neither near enough to the top to have insight into budgeting, and not frequent users of core functionality—"one of the challenges for the IT organization is sensitizing this type of customer to the price associated with the services he or she uses."[1] An effective IT group will ensure that its *relationship* with the relationship customers is built on transparency while shielding them from too much tech-speak.

The final classification of customers is IT influencers. This group may be expending political capital to support IT initiatives. For them to do so, they need absolute assurance that the Technology group can deliver. A classic IT influencer is "a business-side senior executive, external to the IT organization, who can help develop visions, marshal resources, influence decisions, and [who] is critical for the success of any project."[1] This recommendation removes the chief technology officer from consideration. Some firms may view the CIO as a hybrid role spanning the business and Technology, while others—typically those who also have a chief technology officer—see it as a business-side role. A chief marketing officer comes to mind as a useful champion for CRM. This C-level executive is likely to be (at least somewhat) predisposed to understand the importance of customer centricity, even if he or she is disconnected from the frontline sales portion of the population which also interacts with CRM.

Chief marketing officers may be under pressure from other executives to focus more on analytics than operational CRM, making it even more critical to educate chief marketing officers on the relationship between effective operational CRM and useful analytics. Regardless of which influencers are ultimately identified, once they are in the mix, we must keep them happy. In fact, even one dissatisfied IT influencer can sway senior management's perception of IT value.

The goal of this discussion is not to overcomplicate the interactions between Technology and the business, but rather to sensitize both groups to the complexities inherent to their broader relationship. The business needs to understand the many factors affecting Technology's decisions. At the same time, Technology needs to tailor its products, support and messaging to the various business groups. At the end of the day, "IT operates in an environment in which every perturbation in service becomes the subject of 'watercooler' gossip"[1] and successfully aligning its product and service offerings with its various customer groups will go a long way toward turning those watercooler conversations into forums for praise rather than criticism.

Chapter Summary

In this chapter, we examined the importance of selling the IT function to the business. This is a multifaceted challenge, and it involves the identification and segmentation of internal customers so that solutions can be most appropriately tailored to these customers. The IT function should work to shift the prevailing paradigm of the division as a cost center to an orientation which demonstrates clear value that IT contributes to revenue generation activities. The Technology Division can benefit by working to increase visibility of technology projects, improving the stability and reliability of its systems, promoting technical literacy, and positioning top tech management personnel as closely as possible to business leaders.

If Technology chooses to embrace a marketing lens and treat itself like a competitor in the marketplace, business units will need to retain appropriate perspective on exactly what is reasonable for Technology to do and not do. If organizations find themselves continually choosing external options in favor of their own colleagues, they should immediately look to supplement funding and resources for the Technology Division to ensure that it has equal footing to compete as well as preserve the morale of employees.

References

1. Hirschheim, R., Schwarz, A., & Todd, P. (2006). A marketing maturity model for IT: Building a customer-centric IT organization. *IBM Systems Journal 45(1)*, 181–197.
2. Higgins, P. E., & Halvorson, P. H. (2013). *Focus: Use Different Ways of Seeing the World for Success and Influence.* New York: Plume and The Penguin Group.
3. Ang, L., & Buttle, F. (2006). CRM software applications and business performance. *Database of Marketing & Customer Strategy Management 14*, 4–16.

7

Developing a CRM Governance Model

Corporate governance of information technology (IT) is a broad topic and is the subject of countless studies. We can glean a number of insights from these studies and leverage them to guide our implementation of a customer relationship management (CRM) governance structure. We do not presuppose that all readers are positioned to create a governance structure, but robust understanding of the governance principles outlined in this chapter will help make existing governance models more effective. If we take away an understanding of how governance structures can succeed and fail along with guidance on how to approach the members of your existing governance committee, we will be better positioned to effect change.

In a study, Raghupathi defined IT governance as "the leadership and organizational structures and processes that ensure IT sustains and extends the organization's strategies and objectives."[1] We could extend and provide additional specificity by defining governance as a corporate structure that provides oversight, facilitates decision-making, and ensures accountability surrounding the intended strategy, execution, and management of IT. The need for effective IT governance at the broad organizational level is critical, and the effective governance of CRM is an important component that contributes to CRM success.

The participants in the governance process have a straightforward—if not always simple—mission. They "seek to minimize technology costs, while ensuring that the infrastructure can accommodate increasing utilization, new software applications, and modifications to existing software applications."[2] The effective execution of governance initiatives can have myriad benefits. At its best, "quality [Information Technology Governance] influences ethical practices and corporate awareness of the environment and societal interests of the communities in which they operate."[1] The notion of scalability is present within the definition of governance, as is the notion of cost control, which has long been a priority for the Technology Division. As we examined in the previous chapter, however, this orientation has caused some organizations to render their IT division prostrate, and the time has come for a paradigm shift. As we review the current governance literature, however, the cost-cutting focus for IT remains dominant.

IT governance is a descendent of traditional corporate governance, which focused on risk mitigation, reputational concerns, and other high-level items and was handled by corporate boards of directors. These folks typically did not get involved in operational issues, yet as IT emerged as the backbone of operational considerations, boards found themselves with increasing responsibilities which they handled with varying levels of competence. The level of competence and understanding both of boards and also of other internal governance structures must improve as it pertains to the Technology function. Indeed, despite the necessity of thorough and thoughtful technology governance,

> such oversight is often delegated to lower management as operations matters, more an overhead item than a primary factor of production.... Faced with technology issues for which they have little interest and even less expertise, boards have largely left [Information Technology Governance] on the sidelines.[1]

As we can see, there are numerous opportunities for missteps in the development of a governance model. Before firms proceed too far along in a governance initiative, they will be best suited by developing a very clear picture of what they hope to achieve with their governance structure and how it benefits the organization. When lobbying with boards, the translation of technical speak to business speak will be especially important. Boards will not spend time and effort on technology governance if they do not unequivocally understand the benefits.

Practical Importance and Efficacy

The academic literature clearly demonstrates the importance of IT governance, and this position was underscored by the CRM experts interviewed for this book, who were adamant about the importance of a strong CRM governance model and who emphasized that the role of such a structure should be well understood and not limited to data governance. To that end, Tim Kippley of Rightpoint Consulting noted:

> One thing that I think firms are becoming more aware of is that governance goes beyond data. People would come to us and want to talk about data stewardship and data governance. And that's very important to a CRM system, sure. To us, we want to cover all the bases. I like to treat [CRM] like a product. Governance covers features, it covers how the organization is staffed to support the system. That can go from people who are trained to be more experts to be specialized in certain areas all the way down to people who understand how to maintain more basic elements.[3]

Kippley's comments underscore the reality that governance is very important not just for data quality or ensuring system stability but also as a mechanism for driving adoption and for adding value to the system. He notes just as consumer products release features which we often did not realize we wanted until we see them, CRM systems can strive to predict users' future needs. While aspirational for some companies that have viewed governance mostly in a data context, Kippley believes that the more we can focus on governance as a channel through which the system can continually evolve and adapt, the greater value we will realize throughout our CRM initiatives. The importance of a robust governance structure was referenced in a 2016 interview with another prominent CRM implementation expert, who noted:

> Not having a CRM governance structure is huge mistake. You can call it what you want—governance team, center of excellence. But if you don't have that, you're not going to effective at rolling out CRM programs. You're not going to be as controlled. You'll end up with many disparate groups operating in completely disparate ways.[4]

Organizational resistance to governance structures is a common frustration among practitioners. After all, the whole idea of a governance team is to have a central command center of sorts to guide business decisions and implement features in a timely manner, share best practices, and control the levels of customization to ensure long-term system viability. The consultant cited above further noted that having the governance hierarchy in place allows valuable oversight in the context of phasing rollouts effectively and lamented the reality that he sees so many clients who are adverse to this structure. "It's disheartening to think they just want to get right to it but they're not being *strategic* about it after making this huge investment in CRM. They're missing out on the benefits of CRM by being disconnected and not joined together by a governance team."[4]

Governance Models

Our challenge when developing a governance model is to create a structure through which influencers may have their voices heard while simultaneously providing the means to filter out the noise. In other words, some folks may have strong personal opinions which should not necessarily be actioned. We should endeavor, however, to create an environment in which everyone feels his voice can be heard, even if his input is not congruent with the broader group's consensus. One of the most important considerations of ensuring governance actors' participation is by choosing the governance *structure* best suited to an organization's strengths and weaknesses.

Governance structures can be fundamentally centralized or decentralized. To the former, "the primary argument for centralized IT governance is that influential managers are involved in making IT decisions."[2] One of the largest risks involved in implementing a centralized IT governance structure is the risk of top management micromanaging. The second risk is the marginalization of end-user contributions. The latter risk can be mitigated by the creation of a user contribution committee, which could include—depending on an organization's size—up to a dozen end users spanning multiple levels of experience in the organization.

Decentralized governance comes with its own benefits and drawbacks. To the latter, for example, "when decision authority is decentralized, IT professionals (while close to the problem) may not understand the negative effects of their ideal 'local' solution on other areas of the firm."[2] That effect can be mitigated by clear alignment between functional areas. The counterpoint is an extension of our concern about senior management muddling, which could disempower local managers, even though they almost certainly possess a greater understanding of the issues at hand. A decentralized model also reduces the risk of information overload, analysis paralysis, and unnecessary complexity.

This is a debate analogous to the one faced by the founding fathers of the United States: centralized federal power or allotment of many decisions to the states. When it comes to IT governance, different enterprise technology systems may benefit from different structures. In a 2014 study, Thompson, Ekman, Selby, and Whitaker, however, found that for CRM, a top-down centralized model may not be the best course. The study concluded that "distinctive characteristics of CRM data processing and the localized nature of CRM efforts are best supported when CRM technologies are loosely coupled to the broader infrastructure and governed locally."[2] The key difference between the centralized and decentralized models is the influence of—you guessed it—top management. Given how much we have highlighted the importance of top management in a CRM initiative, it might seem intuitively that the findings of the above study must be flawed. After all, if top management is more closely involved in the CRM governance process, the initiative cannot help but succeed. We must here draw a distinction between the various mechanisms by which top management can participate in a CRM initiative.

We have seen evidence advocating both centralized and decentralized structures. As practitioners, we will need to have a pulse of the organization. Are users notoriously underrepresented while senior managers pick into every little detail? We might then consider lobbying for decentralized governance. If senior management strikes the correct posture of advocacy and the organization understands the importance of users being represented even at dialogues at the highest organizational levels, centralized governance might be a viable option. Ultimately, the challenge falls to us to evaluate the organizational culture and climate, and make recommendations about the best course of governance.

Actors

One of the most common and useful governance structures is the steering committee, which is useful to gain support of business representatives, but which risks loss of user input as its key weakness unless it is architected effectively. The steering committee should not consider itself bound only to CRM initiatives. While some of the committee members will have a sales or marketing focus, an effective steering committee will also include folks with a pulse on the broader organization. We should look for every opportunity to increase knowledge of the specific technology being used to support CRM among steering committee members and their colleagues, being cognizant that it is important for these well-positioned persons to "bring CRM technology deeper into strategies, employees, business processes and resource configuration, in addition to technology advancement."[5] CRM expert Tim Kippley opined on the appropriate composition of the governance team:

> [You want to include] the business in general. At a tactical level they're the ones who understand the data. To make decisions about certain information, you really do need people to say "that's just not right, because I know xyz company is structured this way".
>
> At a strategic level it's all about buy-in. I'm not saying the CEO needs to be but the business lines need to be heavily involved but individuals who represent the business lines need to be heavily involved in the structure. Also, Administrative personnel and IT are important contributors. [At the same time, governance committees] can get too big and they can get over-engineered. As broad and aspirational as I was, we always want to think big, act small. That applies to an implementation and also how you address governance. Don't over-complicate it. Keep it focused on your key goals. But guard against it because they can get engineered and overblown very quickly.[3]

We can see that multiple perspectives are critical to making a governance model successful. Extrapolating on Kippley's recommendations, we can gain additional clarity about the specific perspectives each group brings to the table within a governance structure. We will now evaluate several groups of employees and how their relative contributions can influence positive outcomes.

Top Management

Top management best serves CRM with their voice, advocacy, and focus on CRM's importance and the imperative to utilize technology and embrace the customer-centric strategy. The role—if interpreted as we have—has virtually no place within a governance model primarily concerned with making CRM decisions. Management is, unfortunately, too often disconnected from the grassroots factors that should influence implementation decisions. This is not limited to CRM governance. In a 2007 study, Raghupathi examining a broader IT governance found a "basic disconnect between boards and the IT staffs of the companies they oversee."[1] In an effort to embrace top management support however they can get it, some firms have allowed the pendulum to swing too far in the direction of senior management. Perhaps having read some of the very studies we have cited in this text, firms implore top management to be intimately involved in the CRM governance process. This is not the right approach. Top management is—unless properly educated on an ongoing basis—far too disconnected from day-to-day system use to make decisions about core functionality, which necessitates a voice from the user community.

Some might argue that we are cherry-picking, asking top management to be toothless cheerleaders. It might well be that many folks' personalities would not allow that, and they could hardly help themselves from dipping into the details. For those managers with strong technical literacy, this might not be a concern. A senior manager with strong technical acumen could be a powerful ally in the governance process, but only if he listens carefully to his user base and is not heavy handed with his proposals. One of the most misguided influencers in the governance process is the person who knows just enough about technology to be dangerous. These folks may be likely to dream up pet projects with little relevance to the most pressing issues at hand. When these individuals are identified, the CRM team must use their political capital and negotiation skills to ensure that a manager's pet project does not derail a CRM initiative from its core objectives. Managers should be encouraged to be champions and not be loaded down in implementation details. Regardless of which structure you choose to implement, it is useful to select employees who are good listeners to be key participants. A governance committee is ripe for diatribes and fertile ground for those who enjoy hearing themselves speak. Those in charge of planning each meeting must be especially adept at keeping people on topic, creating formal agendas and sticking to them.

Support Team

Some firms have incorrectly categorized system support roles as inferior to project management roles—until it is time for downsizing, during which they wise up and protect the folks who keep the systems running. Support teams must be well integrated into the governance structure, for they receive much user feedback. If a governance structure omits or undervalues the support team, the team will feel disempowered and ultimately provide lower quality service Failing to provide this integration creates an environment where everyone loses: support teams and users become angry and frustrated, and management fails to hear the voices of the users, which in turn results in poor decision-making, which results in frustrated users with increased support needs—and thus the cycle repeats itself.

Everyone in the governance structure should carry an equal vote, including the support representative. He should bring a couple of user-driven requests to each meeting and lobby for their prioritization. The criticality of this role has gained attention in some academic literature suggesting that this role, which acts as an intermediary between the Technology Division and business units, has become more popular recently. This reality will be explored further in our chapter on support. Such direct contact with the user base is useful, and it necessitates the presence of the support liaison at the governance table. Hirschheim, Schwarz, and Todd underscored the importance of inclusion from the support team in a 2006 study that "the enduring nature of the position suggests that there is merit for its inclusion within a corporate IT governance arrangement."[6]

Marketing Management

The marketing function—the natural champions of CRM—has another vote at the table. We would expect the marketing representative to be the most vocal champion of customer centricity, contributing to discussions surrounding the manner in which various governance decisions propel or hinder a customer-oriented culture. Marketing may be less familiar with the intricacies of the sales force automation component, which can at times place them at a different vantage point. An effective marketing representative can see moments when enhancements may not be flashy or advance the marketing agenda but which are nevertheless required for operational efficiency and effectiveness. It is the responsibility of sales management to provide the justification for those initiatives that are focused more on SFA in particular.

Sales Management

Sales management should—even outside of the formal governance structure—maintain a close relationship with the support representative to ensure that management has a pulse on the user community and their concerns. Sales management should present proposals for system enhancements to improve customer identification, segmentation, and retention along with operational improvement requests such as business process efficiency analyses and technical improvements. They also generally look for business intelligence in the form of dashboards and reports. Each type of request is important. In scenarios where management represents management instead of frontline sales, the manager will often find himself at odds with the support representative, who will question the lack of perspective and equality of proposals.

Technology

Technology may be, in some firms, underrepresented in a governance structure, but this decision is to the firm's peril, as underscored in a 2012 study by S. Dong who noted that "the execution of decisions on complex, multidivisional business applications such as CRM systems requires significantly high levels of *both* centralized top management support and decentralized collaboration between business and IT managers."[5] This research suggests that the governance structure should hear perhaps not from the very top of the technology personnel hierarchy but from someone who has a balanced view of the technical challenges as well as broader business implications. At the same time, empowering IT leadership to engage more effectively at all levels is most certainly worth pursuing.

Chapter Summary

In this chapter, we have explored the importance of implementing a robust CRM governance model. Historically, governance challenges resulted from lack of technical acumen on the part of senior managers, which led to misalignment and undesirable outcomes. As organizations mature and increase their technical acumen, senior managers are better positioned to make contributions. We now also understand that the successful governance model includes broad representation from business units, the Technology Division, senior management, and the support team.

We have learned that governance models can be either centralized or decentralized. Some evidence suggests that a highly centralized model may disempower local managers who likely are better positioned to articulate problems and propose solutions. Centralized models provide the risk of increased top management muddling. The role of top management must be managed, and a delicate balance must be struck between specific management contributions and broad, generalized advocacy. Ultimately, practitioners must make decisions as to what they believe best aligns with organizational culture and climate.

We understand that governance is about so much more than ensuring data quality but also is a critical mechanism to ensure organizational excellence, provide controls and regulations on changes to CRM, and provide a forum for all parties involved in the CRM process to come together and look for areas of common ground. Those parties should represent a wide swath of those who touch CRM, including sales management, marketing management, the Technology Division, and relevant business units.

References

1. Raghupathi, W. (2007). Corporate governance of IT: A framework for development. *Communications of the ACM 50(8)*, 94–99.

2. Thompson, S., Ekman, P., Selby, D., & Whitaker, J. (2014). A model to support IT infrastructure planning and the allocation of IT governance authority. *Decision Support Systems 59*, 108–118.
3. Kippley, T., & Schneider, B. (2016, February 18). CRM practitioners—Rightpoint. (S. J. Kinnett, Interviewer).
4. Anonymous. (2016, January 12–13). Making CRM successful—CRM practitioner interview. (S. J. Kinnett, Interviewer).
5. Dong, S. (2012). Decision execution mechanisms of IT governance: The CRM case. *International Journal of Information Management 32*, 147–157.
6. Hirschheim, R., Schwarz, A., & Todd, P. (2006). A marketing maturity model for IT: Building a customer-centric IT organization. *IBM Systems Journal 45(1)*, 181–197.

PART II

IMPLEMENTATION

8

PARTNERS, VENDORS, AND HOSTED SOLUTIONS

Building a customer-centric organization and a customer relationship management (CRM) strategy are in the purest sense technologically agnostic initiatives. As we have begun to explore, however, there is a circular relationship between technology and strategy. The strategy shapes the technology; the technology shapes the strategy. This counter-intuitive relationship has often been overlooked or denied during the build versus buy evaluation. Cost concerns, time-to-market pressures, and lack of robust internal information technology (IT) resources have led many firms to embrace packaged software, yet this decision has often painted them into a corner. Ten years ago, the build versus buy dilemma was a very real one, but as of the writing of this book, most firms have accepted the need for packaged CRM solutions. To that end, Tim Kippley, CRM Practice Lead at Rightpoint Consulting, Chicago, said:

> That war is almost over in the CRM space. I would be really surprised if a firm says they can build a CRM better than those in the marketplace. Other technologies are more nascent. People aren't asking for a build or buy assessment today for CRM systems. The customization battle within a packaged system is still there but the build or buy decision is essentially solved.[1]

This point was further underscored by a leading CRM consultant, who—after disclosing his evangelism for a particular software product—said that even taking his particular preferences off the table, he advocated firms selecting packaged solutions, noting some firms may not require much tailoring of these systems to meet their business processes. When pressed on the issue, he admitted that "if a client says he want to do XYZ in an application but doesn't want to use it as it's built, I would agree they would be better off with an in-house solution."[2] Assuming organizations heed the general advice to use packaged CRM solutions, they still have important decisions to make in what packaged system they select and who they will enlist to help them with implementation. In this chapter, we will discuss psychological, technical, and financial considerations that firms should review when making these decisions.

Psychological Considerations

When members of an organization first hear about an impending packaged software implementation, a number of phenomena begin to occur. The first is a natural psychological reaction called *not invented here (NIH)*, "an organizational phenomenon in which groups resist ideas and inputs from external sources, often resulting in subpar performance and redundant effort."[3] The underlying causes of NIH could result from a perception that external vendors are profit-driven rather than customer-driven and that they could not possibly understand all of the intricacies of the business. In a similar vein, the Technology Division may see the buy decision as a direct affront to its competence, despite how mature and sophisticated the packaged CRM industry has become. While completely eliminating such a visceral phenomenon as NIH might not be realistic, with proper change management processes and appropriate implementation of partner selection, the phenomenon can be mitigated. To the point of perception management, we do see some evidence of this challenge in the literature, with a 2006 study noting that "one of the main concerns with adopting CRM [packaged] software is that it is perceived to come in a 'one size fits all' package."[4] That perception had not changed by 2010 as reported in a study of enterprise software deployment in the manufacturing industry, which noted that "[Enterprise System] literature explicitly acknowledges that an ES package is unlikely to include all the functionality an organization needs."[5] That often necessitates the need to customize the software and develop integration points with other systems. While packaged software can always be customized, the level and sophistication of customization vary from vendor to vendor. Some packaged software may be more difficult to customize. There is some benefit to limited customization. In some cases, the technology may actually help firms to improve their existing practices and gain new efficiencies, which we will explore in greater depth in a subsequent chapter. Out-of-the box functionality has been honed and refined through many iterations to reflect a consensus-based set of tools. The successes and failures of various implementation methods have been—we would presume—taken into account. One harsh reality of packaged software, however, is that sometimes even it does not get it right.

We can see that individual and group psychologies can be influenced by the decision to purchase a packaged product instead of building one in-house. Psychological factors are often the most obtrusive and least recognized collection of factors comprising the build or buy decision, which is why they are listed here first. It is important to remember that there may be many reasons why a firm would believe that the NIH challenge is worth the cost savings or perceived reliability of a packaged solution. By simply being aware of the potential cognitive impacts of implementing packaged software, we can go a long way toward adapting a positioning strategy to drive adoption. Packaged products do certainly bring certain advantages but the psychological challenges they bring to firms are real.

The Partner–Vendor Paradigm

Another psychological factor, which will play a critical role in the success of a CRM implementation is the posture an organization takes toward its implementation provider. Words matter, and defining the relationship you have with your consultants will help build a paradigm for engagement. A leading CRM consultant noted:

> There are always different personalities at play but in general there are two types of clients. There are clients that treat a strategic implementation provider as a vendor and other clients who treat them as a partner. A lot of times it's cultural, it may have to do with the type of organization, where they're headquartered, but if we're treated as a vendor, clients often draw hard lines, spend a lot of time spinning wheels, trying to connect and communicate a perspective. But when they're treated as a partner, they hold the implementation team's perspective and experiences and best practices in high regard. I've been in both situations. When I've been treated as a vendor, clients spend so much time, wasting

time, going in circles, instead of giving weight to the best practices and perspectives of a CRM team who does this for a living, day-in, day out, and that approach results in a much more positive collaboration rather than taking a hard line.[2]

This partner versus vendor paradigm is about more than labels and could be considered one of the most fundamental principles to CRM success. Nurturing a strong relationship between your implementation partners does not just make for a smoother and better implementation environment, but it also has real impacts on end-user acquisition of CRM technical skills. To that end, a 2011 study found a "positive significant relationship between the constructs of external ERP expertise and business employees' skills when in-house IT knowledge is factored in as a mediator."[6] This suggests that effective internal IT staff act as a bridge between those who are technically challenged within their organization and external implementation partners, facilitating effective knowledge transfer.

Not only does this speak to the importance of strong knowledge sharing between implementation partners and internal IT staff but also it suggests high-caliber IT staff will have a direct impact on CRM success by acting as a knowledge bridge. While this may sound obvious—which firm does not want the best employees?—we continue to see evidence of IT cost cutting. An additional study conducted by Hirschheim, Schwarz, and Todd in 2006 found that the "the advent of enterprise software has significantly blurred the line between application and infrastructure and has complicated the division of activities between internal and external providers of IT for organizations."[7] A well-functioning, partner instead of vendor, relationship will improve employee alignment and, as a result, work to reduce the ambiguity in role responsibility and reduce role conflict.

Parallels to Business–IT Alignment and Technology Positioning

We can see parallels between the partner–vendor paradigm and business–IT alignment. Organizations with a one-way relationship between business units and Technology find themselves in an analogous position to the posture of treating external implementation providers as vendors rather than partners. This manifests itself in the prescriptive manner in which business units may approach Technology. Rather than sharing the broader business context and goals surrounding a particular request, they may instead—subconsciously viewing Technology as a commodity meant to execute on isolated requests— ask for piecemeal changes such as adding a new checkbox on a screen.

In scenarios where the Technology Division has not demonstrated competency (the first tier of the competency–credibility–commitment model we examined in our chapter on positioning the Technology Division), the division will have less success influencing business users to break out of the vendor paradigm and moving to a partnership posture. Finding opportunities to make the Technology Division more visible through mechanisms such as embedded engineers, open prioritization meetings, and feedback sessions will be useful to the ongoing positioning and alignment challenges. Face-to-face contact will be most effective, followed by calls then emails. Representatives from Technology should not be shy about explaining the reasoning behind requests for broader business context rather than blind execution of business requests. Showing that the requests are not pushback but rather discussions surrounding these requests actually enables the Technology Division to develop more strategic long-term solutions and add greater value to the business. These considerations can, when pursued over time, gently move the needle to a more productive business–IT relationship.

Technical Considerations and Hosted Solutions

As of the writing of this book, in 2016, firms have shown demonstrably decreased appetite for building in-house CRM solutions and increased appetite for packaged CRM solutions and in particular cloud computing solutions now named "software as a service" (SaaS). Cloud computing refers to "virtual servers, distributed hosting in large datacenters, and shared resources available over the internet."[8] One survey of chief information officers (CIOs) conducted by Barwick in 2014 found that SaaS CRM solutions had been implemented by 23% of firms whose CIOs were surveyed, but that in terms of total IT activities, SaaS solutions accounted for only 13%. These data suggest that CRM systems eclipse the general IT landscape as candidates for SaaS. The specific reasoning for these decisions may have to do with the quality of packaged solutions along with the nature of CRM data. Firms may be more reluctant, for example, to store their financial books and records outside of their own infrastructure. CRM functionality may also be more apt to succeed in a thin-client, SaaS environment than other systems. Regardless of specific reasons, the robust marketing of many successful SaaS solutions can make SaaS solutions seem as if they are dominating the market. While we have seen market share continue to grow, SaaS solutions remain the proverbial "new kid on the block."

Hosted solutions could be more vulnerable than their in-house counterparts when it comes to security, being more exposed to the risk of hackers. Business continuity is another concern. Hosted service providers are relatively new in our industry and few have been tested over the long haul. If a provider—for example—went out of business, a firm would be placed in an extremely stressful position as it scrambles to replace the provider. Cloud computing might not be a good solution for firms who need rapid system response time. Folks taking inbound calls, for example, who must stall callers and rely on their small talk skills while they watch a spinning wheel on their web browser, would be made understandably miserable from a cloud-based thin-client solution unless the system was, against the odds, sufficiently fast. A cloud-based solution would be more palatable in an environment with infrequent searches and in scenarios where customers are not waiting for information housed within the CRM to be retrieved. If firms in these environments are keen to use cloud solutions for other reasons, establishing assertive service level agreements for system response time would be beneficial.

Financial and Managerial Considerations

Financial considerations are, as we might imagine, also relevant to firms' CRM decisions. Some of the most popular market solutions are also very expensive, despite the initial promise of SaaS to be a means to save money. To that end, one of the seminal arguments in favor of SaaS solutions was purported streamlined upgrading and fewer in-house technologists required to develop enhancements. The validity of this argument is contingent—as with any packaged software solution—on the level of customization that has been implemented. In fact, during implementations with high levels of customization, bringing CRM implementation specialists back under new support contracts to handle required upgrades and ongoing business requirements will further increase the cost of keeping CRM running. As packaged SaaS solutions bring more and more features to the table and adjust pricing models to reflect the additional features, firms have reason to be skeptical that purely financial incentives are what drive the packaged software selection decision. Furthermore, the supply of quality implementation specialists, while growing, has not reached a point where they have lost competitive pricing. Taking the above in the aggregate, firms can benefit from understanding that the literal price tag on the packaged CRM solution is one of the many financial components required to achieve CRM success.

Managerial considerations are also important in understanding the packaged CRM decision-making landscape. For example, a 2012 study of firms across the world found that "in the past couple of years, business agility and speed to market has moved up from the mid-teens to within the top five management concerns."[9] Speed to market is one of the primary benefits provided by a packaged software solution and particularly a hosted solution, which utilizes existing firm infrastructure (i.e., Internet browsers and network connections). Firms should do what they can to build the strongest environment they can, focusing on infrastructure, stability, and speed in order to maximize their chances of benefiting from SaaS.

Finally, managers should take pause if their primary driver to moving to a vendor solution is to mitigate the impacts of outsourcing or downsizing, as these drivers pose the greatest risk to CRM success given that the sophistication of the in-house IT function is so critical to an effective packaged software implementation. A study on ERP implementations highlights this reality, advising management to be sure that in-house IT personnel "are able to provide assistance to other organizational members when complex IT systems such as ERP are being acquired."[6] In addition to providing some mitigating relief to the NIH phenomenon, which organically occurs during all vendor product acquisitions, in-house IT personnel are more likely to build relationships with other business users during the implementation phase and are increasingly likely to elicit positive adoption outcomes. Firms that have or may be considering IT outsourcing initiatives should take great pause upon noting these results.

Chapter Summary

Hosted, packaged software solutions are increasingly found to be popular within the CRM space, having grown steadily over the past several years. The purported benefits of such products include speed to market, reduced operational overhead costs, and easy customization. When evaluating these decisions, firms should examine technical, psychological, and financial considerations. The decision to purchase packaged, externally hosted, software can have cultural implications resulting from a psychological phenomenon known as NIH. Hosted CRM solutions remain a promising option for many organizations, though the majority of the firms have yet to pursue such initiatives. Firms considering a packaged CRM implementation with the aim of reducing in-house IT resources should understand that in-house IT plays a number of critical roles in the CRM implementation process, which translate to real results especially in the context of user adoption. The financial implications of hosted CRM solutions include ongoing licensing costs and ongoing maintenance either by internal IT or external implementation partners.

Given the complexity of hosted solutions, we understand that we will invariably need the aid of consultants or specialists with expertise in the particular piece of packaged software we choose. We have seen that it is not only the proper selection of these consultants, which is important, but also the manner in which we engage them. Even decisions about whether consultants should have company email addresses or be engaged through their consulting firm's email accounts contribute to the posture, which will be assumed not only by internal implementation resources but also end users themselves. We would strongly encourage firms to onboard external implementation partners as if they were employees, avoiding terms like "contingent worker" or "temp." The NIH phenomenon applies not only to systems but also to humans and effective management of the phenomenon has real impacts on CRM success.

References

1. Kippley, T., & Schneider, B. (2016, February 18). CRM practitioners—Rightpoint (S. J. Kinnett, Interviewer).
2. Anonymous. (2016, January 12–13). Making CRM successful—CRM practitioner interview (S. J. Kinnett, Interviewer).
3. Lidwell, W., Holden, K., & Butler, J. (2010). *Universal Principles of Design*. Beverly, MA: Rockport.
4. Ang, L., & Buttle, F. (2006). CRM software applications and business performance. *Database of Marketing & Customer Strategy Management 14*, 4–16.
5. Strong, D. M., & Volkoff, O. (2010, December). Understanding organization-enterprise system fit: A path to theorizing the information technology artifact. *MIS Quarterly 34(4)*, 731–756.
6. Ifinedo, P. (2011). Examining the influences of external expertise and in-house computer/IT knowledge on ERP system success. *The Journal of Systems and Software 84*, 2065–2078.
7. Hirschheim, R., Schwarz, A., & Todd, P. (2006). A marketing maturity model for IT: Building a customer-centric IT organization. *IBM Systems Journal 45(1)*, 181–197.
8. Bibi, S., Katsaros, D., & Bozanis, P. (2012). Business application acquisition: On-premise or SaaS-based solutions. *IEEE Software 29(3)*, 86–92.
9. Luftman, J., Zadeh, S. H., Derksen, B., Santana, M., Rigoni, E. H., & Huang, Z. D. (2012). Key information technology and management issues 2011–2012: An international study. *Journal of Information Technology 27*, 198–212.

9
THE BUSINESS ANALYSIS FUNCTION

Once implementation partners have been selected and onboarded, we next begin to focus on requirements elicitation and the business analysis function. The International Institute for Business Analysis, cited by Kathleen B. Hass in her book *Professionalizing Business Analysis: Breaking the Cycle of Challenged Projects*, published the results of research conducted by Forester who found "poorly defined applications have led to a persistent miscommunication between business and IT that largely contributes to a 66% project failure rate for these applications, costing U.S. businesses at least $30B every year."[1] Such ambiguities in definitions and the subsequent miscommunication across business and the Technology Division reminds us of our discussion of business–IT alignment—a persistent challenge for firms, which may become most apparent during projects and in particular during the business analysis process.

While a thorough treatment of all phases of the development life cycle is out of the scope of this book, given the existing research surrounding the criticality of the business analysis function, an examination of this function can aid firms in achieving customer relationship management (CRM) success. Failing to adequately master the business analysis function is a large handicap that will cause firms to risk project failure right from the beginning of the project. Every staffing decision is important but Hass reminds us that "without well-understood and well-documented requirements, it is virtually impossible to meet project objectives"[1] and even in an environment of scarce resources and budget, requirements definition and management should be the stage of the development life cycle receiving the most support.

To begin with, one business analyst might not be enough for large projects. It is not only the quantity of business analysts that is of such import but also how they are spending their time. The many respon-sibilities placed on most business analysts are decreasing the quality of the core business analysis function—the very function shown to be so critical to the success of system implementations. Hass, noted above, outlines a breakdown of the typical business analyst's respon-sibilities, suggesting that true business analysis represents 29.3% of the total job requirements. Note that very activity which gives the position its name does not even exceed half of its total allocation. Hass notes that business analysts are required to perform many differ-ent activities besides business analysis including engineering, design, and project management and that business analysts are often assigned to multiple projects at once. Given all of the challenges surrounding CRM implementation and the demonstrated importance of the busi-ness analysis function, Hass recommends all such high-risk projects should be staffed by a senior business analyst dedicated full time to one project with no other responsibilities.

In situations where a business analyst role is merged with both a technical lead and project manager role, Hass writes that the nature of technical activities will occupy most of the individual's time and sum-marizes the point directly: "Make no mistake: using the same person as a technical lead, project manager, and business analyst has con-tributed significantly to challenged and failed projects."[1] Many firms may be aware of this reality but could argue that budget constraints tie their hands. Indeed, we have pointed to and will continue to point to several areas where organizations can be apt to under-resource and thus put themselves at risk for poor outcomes. Ultimately, the cumulative focus on these myriad items of importance may suggest that many existing budgeting models are idealistic but not realistic. Because of the front-loaded nature of the business analysis function, and the importance of starting any project, CRM or otherwise, on the right foot, we must be honest with ourselves about just how important the business analysis function is and the risks of underestimating that importance as manifested by resourcing decisions.

Competency Alignment

As noted above, business analysts in the modern enterprise often perform functions diametrically opposed to each other. Project management is an entirely different competency than business analysis and the innate cognitive orientation of intuitive business analysts is not the same as that of natural project managers. From a personnel perspective, this will be a hard sell: a request for two new headcount instead of one. For firms willing to trust the recommendation of separating the project management function from the business analysis function, they will find over time that they have employees operating to their strengths. When operating as another of the groups of people who provide updates to the project managers, rather than being those managers themselves, business analysts will have an opportunity to thrive and expand time outside of requirement sessions to improve their knowledge of the enterprise technology landscape, become more skilled subject matter experts, and evangelize various products.

Positioning

Deciding where the business analyst should reside within the organizational structure is an important consideration with each option bringing consequential ramifications. A number of options exist. A business analyst could sit within the Technology Division, a project management office (PMO), or within a business unit. The first options, reporting up through the Technology Division or a PMO, have the potential to bring a critically important benefit: the ability for business analysts to form what Hass calls *communities of practice*, which facilitate "consistency, standards, improvement of the business analysis process, and advancement of the business analysis profession within the organization."[1] Realizing these benefits will, however, be predicated on how effectively collaboration is practiced as a key value in organizational culture. We will now examine the implications of each positioning decision.

Project Management Office

Placing business analysts within a PMO office may result in clearer career paths than other positioning approaches since managers in PMO may be able to compare and contrast the strengths of one analyst versus another. The latter may result in competition for advancement among the business analysts. While some level of this may be useful, it also creates a fundamentally different environment than either of the other scenarios. Some projects may be more difficult than others in various respects—complexity of requirements, difficulty of user engagement, and many more. Consider the plight of the business analyst assigned to a CRM project.

The PMO must guard against applying one-size-fits-all evaluation criteria, which is easier said than done. This is one reason we recommend against housing business analysts within the PMO. To an earlier point, the communities of practice, which might develop within the PMO environment, while once again useful in theory, may become too cerebral and backfire when proposed in the context of real-life scenarios. Such postures may lead both business units and the Technology Division to perceive business analysts as disconnected, pie in the sky, outsiders out of touch with both business units and the Technology Division.

Business Units

Placing business analysts within business units often seems very attractive on the surface. With their deep integration, they will likely become more familiar with business processes and context, which can subsequently inform their decisions on projects. Hybrid business analyst/support resource roles—while contradicting one of our core assertions about business analyst responsibilities—admittedly provide even greater opportunity to understand the ins and outs of the business. Further, business users may come to feel they have a strong advocate who truly understands them and in whom they have confidence to represent their needs to the Technology Division.

On the other hand, business analysts may become disconnected from the Technology Division. The business analyst may then seek to represent the business without collaborating as much with Technology, given the distance in the relationship. In order to counteract this phenomenon, Hass recommends management within the Technology Division "reach out to the business units to conduct working sessions and ensure that the appropriate business SMEs are fully engaged in decisions regarding IT support, maintenance, and enhancement work."[1]

While the decentralized model of business analysts reporting up through a business unit could help to ensure increased understanding of business needs and facilitate stronger relationships with business stakeholders, these benefits must be weighed against the resulting disconnectedness a business analyst will have with the Technology Division from both relationship and knowledge perspectives. To combat this challenge, Hass again recommends communities of practice as paramount for success.

The career path for decentralized business analysts is also less clear. If a business analyst reported up through, for example, a revenue group like sales, can we really count on compensation decision makers to take care of a business analyst as well as those actually closing deals? These managers are also less likely to understand just how challenging the role is and the benefits it brings to their group. The risk of lower compensation and career ambiguity can discourage many high caliber business analysts from taking jobs in organizations who embrace this decentralized model.

The Technology Division

While positioning decisions will have some dependencies on the rest of an organization's structure and culture, our research and experience lead us to recommend—from a reporting perspective—a centralized model but one in which, despite reporting up to the Technology Division, seats personnel in or adjacent to their business units. This approach, while imperfect, allows significantly stronger career development and reasonable performance evaluations. It also makes business units feel more that their business analysts have a greater understanding of the challenges they face. By retaining a reporting line into the Technology Division, attending team meetings, and staying on top of realities within the technology environment, the business analysts will remain empathetic to business concerns without becoming disconnected from technical realities. This embedding will be especially useful in the context of CRM implementations.

Given salespeople's notorious resistance to outsiders, who they perceive as naïve to the challenges they face, embedded business analysts will provide visible evidence of Technology's commitment to the sales function. Many firms are beginning to find the value of embedding not only business analysts but also support personnel and evangelists within business units while allow these personnel to retain reporting lines to the Technology Division.

Requirements

At the beginning of this chapter, we reviewed a key statistic about the detrimental impact that incomplete or inaccurate requirements can have on projects and, given all the challenges which face us within the CRM space, we seek to leave no stone unturned in our quest to understand every contributor to CRM success and also those which can lead to failure. We begin with a formal definition of business requirements as "the essential conditions or capabilities of the enterprise that must be supported by the business solutions."[1] Note the technical agnosticism of the statement. Often times we think of requirements as system-specific mandates, but really requirements are broader than that. Business solutions almost always include process changes and we can use this definition to inform our approach to CRM.

Business analysis processes have been in use for some time, yet a 2011 study underscored that the business analysis process is much more nuanced than it seems on the surface. To that end, Rogers, Sharp, and Preece noted myriad terminology exists including "requirements gathering, requirements capture, requirements elicitation, requirements analysis, and requirements engineering."[2] Words like gathering and capturing requirements imply such requirements exist, are defined, and can be retrieved with a little detective work. They go on to distinguish these processes from elicitation, which "implies that others (presumably the clients or users) know the requirements and we have to get them to tell us."[2] In practice, many of us have observed a much more fluid environment and understanding these paradigms can help to prepare us as we begin the requirements process. Ultimately, Rogers, Sharp, and Preece suggest the phrase "*establishing requirements* to represent the fact that requirements have been established from a sound understanding of the users' needs and that they can be justified by and related back to the data collected."[2]

Kathleen Hass, whose book has provided the backbone of our discussion, defines the requirements end-to-end process as consisting of the phases:

- Elicitation
- Analysis
- Specification
- Documentation
- Validation

Hass's recommendations are by no means diminished by her choice of wording, and indeed elicitation seems to be the most common paradigm and one which remains informative. We most commonly see the elicitation phase manifested through interviews, surveys, and workshops. Workshops or interviews are perhaps the most widely used. The former allows contributions by teams and allows disagreements to be resolved more quickly than individual interviews. Workshops are efficient and, if the right personnel are involved, provide the opportunity to build relationships between users, managers, and engineers.

Workshops must be supplemented, however, with individual interviews. In the absence of these individual interviews, groupthink might allow workshops to miss nuances in business processes. Complicating this is the reality that some users may be uncomfortable disagreeing with others on their teams—particularly if they are utilizing workarounds such as external spreadsheets or are otherwise lacking mastery in the existing system and its functions. Another limitation of workshops is they tend to capture only what users *believe* they are doing, which may be different, however slightly, from what they are actually doing while sitting in front of their computers. As a result, practitioners can perhaps get the greatest benefit from user shadowing. During our 2016 interview, CRM expert Tim Kippley agreed, noting that user shadowing was—based on his experience—a critical supplement to the workshop approach, not only to capture-specific requirements but also to understand broader business processes and context.

It is understandable that—given time and budget constraints, business analysts may find themselves agreeing with the idea and understanding the benefit of desk visits and user shadowing, but given the nature of the exercise—being able to only shadow one user at a time—they may find themselves gravitating more toward the workshop model. Reinforcing the benefits and criticality of the user-shadowing exercises may help business analysts to lobby project sponsors to allow adequate time to conduct such exercises.

Requirements versus Requests

In a continuation of our circular paradigm of business and technology synergy, it is useful to examine a semantic issue: the implication of requirements. The Agile user story format has addressed—consciously or not—the drawback of thinking about the implementation of business requests as "requirements." We know, going in, that not everyone gets what he wants in the context of CRM implementation. As a result, if we are not able to deliver a business requirement, the implication is abject failure. As we have seen throughout this book, words drive paradigms and facilitating positive paradigms facilitates cross-functional collaboration, an imperative for successful business–IT alignment. The requirements nomenclature also does not exactly foster the sort of partnership type of relationship we want between business units and the Technology Division. Referring to business needs as requests suggests a partnership where the business views its colleagues in Technology as partners, not foot soldiers. The term "requirements" is embedded into the business analysis process and we are not suggesting a simple terminology swap cures all CRM implementation woes. Our purpose here is to reinforce the idea that two-way collaboration between business units and the Technology Division remains critically important.

Chapter Summary

In this chapter, we have examined the business analysis function and its specific criticality among other aspects of a CRM implementation. We have highlighted the importance of providing autonomy to the business analysis function and resisting the temptation to muddy the role with project management or technical design. Research and experience have shown that combining these roles leads to negative outcomes and may even lead organizations to making mistakes during the hiring process as they risk overlooking highly skilled business analysts in lieu of employees who might only be adequate analysts but possess competencies in other areas such as project management. We have learned that we are better securing the aid of an employee with excellent business analysis skills and treat project management and technical design as separate roles.

We have examined a distinction in the way business needs are presented, highlighting the benefits of viewing requirements in a new light—as requests made to the Technology Division, underscoring the partnership necessary between the division and specific business units. We suggest this is a useful paradigm to adopt even if it does not result in specific nomenclature changes within organizations.

References

1. Hass, K. B. (2008). *Professionalizing Business Analysis: Breaking the Cycle of Challenged Projects*. Vienna, VA: Management Concepts, Inc.
2. Rogers, Y., Sharp, H., & Preece, J. (2011). *Interaction Design: Beyond Human–Computer Interaction*. Chichester, West Sussex: Wiley.

10

THE CUSTOMIZATION DEBATE

As customer relationship management (CRM) continues to become the central point for many businesses' operations, the temptation to expand it via customization and configuration has never been higher and paradoxically never so important to guard against. The sheer volume of options offered by many CRM packages—some purport to do everything but pick up your dry cleaning—has led firms to find themselves biting off more than they can chew or becoming mired in analysis paralysis as they seek to evaluate the many options available to them. All packaged software products require configuration to meet each organization's individual needs but it is customization in the form of custom development and screens that does not leverage native functionality against which organizations must be guarded.

The ability to configure CRM in many ways is a hallmark of a strong CRM solution. Configuration means making use of native tools such as user profiles, custom page layouts, security role assignments, and hierarchical relationships. By and large, CRM products accommodate these aspects of implementation without incident. Configuration is always necessary, but the extent of that configuration or the need for customization is a result of either limitations in the packaged solution or factors in the solution that have a negative impact on business processes. While we caution mostly against customization, unstructured configuration changes are not without problems. If changes are not made in a standardized way and well documented, the amount of knowledge needed to maintain the system jumps significantly along with the resources to maintain it though perhaps to a lesser degree than resources needed to support customizations.

Understanding Misfits

We can surmise that most customization proposals have good intentions and at times may be attempts to remedy perceived functionality gaps or limitations in a piece of packaged software. A 2010 study of an ERP implementation in the manufacturing industry conducted by Strong and Volkoff found that scenarios existed where the software was out of alignment with business processes. They characterized these scenarios as *misfits* and proposed that misfits manifest in two key ways: as deficiencies or impositions. They define the former as features not present in the system that are needed. Impositions, on the other hand, result from "inherent characteristics of an [enterprise system] such as integration and standardization"[1] and are considered more serious than deficiencies. Impositions are ironic given that the very characteristics—integration and standardization—which purport many benefits and are often selling points for firms who choose to implement enterprise software systems may well also be the cause of the most serious types of misfits. Impositions may manifest as the system requiring mandatory fields at times in the workflow where the values of these fields would not be known and thus must be populated with dummy data. In general, impositions may introduce required practices that are in conflict with organizational norms, culture, or core processes. This example begins to underscore the criticality of avoiding impositions and acknowledging their greater danger than deficiencies in that impositions "arise from characteristics which are necessarily present in the ES and cannot be eliminated, whereas deficiencies can be resolved through the vendor adding the missing features in subsequent releases or an organization acquiring bolt-on packages to support the needed actions."[1]

The above examples of potential remedies are strong and would be the preferred means to resolve deficiencies. Sometimes vendors may not view a deficiency with the same urgency as one or more of their clients, not have the resources to implement the request, or otherwise be unable to accommodate an initiative to remove the deficiency. A bolt-on package might not be available or might be expensive or have other limitations. These are the scenarios that management wants to address via customization. Tim Kippley of Rightpoint Consulting, Chicago, underscored positive ways to improve your system, noting that packaged software products are not closed solutions and have the potential to be extended in an effective way, suggesting that "you can easily build extensions to them without jeopardizing core strengths. Don't break those, but you can build an add-on module that could help with, for example, the quoting process. That includes user experience, design and the actual wiring up of the user interface then connecting it to the system."[2] Kippley noted that the ability to implement these types of extensions underscores CRM's position as a platform solution. Both deficiencies and impositions, while initially frustrating, provide the opportunity to improve business processes and enforce process discipline.

Opportunities for Process Improvement

In some cases, core features of enterprise systems can actually contribute to an evolution in business processes. Savvy developers of enterprise systems may well have refined their approach to performing a given function after reviewing many implementations. A mature enterprise software package should have incorporated lessons learned from prior versions and deployments. At times, however, firms—and end users in particular—are inclined to believe their practices are superior and the software system is out of alignment. Sometimes they are right, but any time we observe perceived imposition misfits, we should keep an open mind and consider whether the mechanism employed by the system to handle a given business scenario may actually yield a process improvement and, if so, we should consider whether it makes sense to modify our existing business processes. On a related note, when packaged software seems to present with a number of deficiencies— keeping in theme with comments elsewhere in the book—firms could benefit from a process review to identify opportunities to streamline business functions prior to attempting to plug deficiencies with extensive customization. A leading CRM practitioner underscored these points during a 2016 interview, noting:

> It's critical that when you're implementing CRM, you're reevaluating your business processes and confirming they are still valid. When you work on a new implementation, you see so many broken processes, so many workarounds because the old system doesn't make sense. You have

to challenge the business and say: "Do we need to be taking this extra step? Do we need this in the CRM?" When you do challenge, [the business] often says: "We never thought of that. If we don't have to fill out the form this way and we can use the system instead, we will." So there's a lot of opportunity [to improve processes] as long as you challenge the status quo.[3]

This sentiment brings us back to the larger alignment themes discussed in Chapter 4. When effective employee alignment has been achieved, organizations are positioned to embrace challenges to the status quo and respond to them effectively. When business units are misaligned, warnings from consultants or the Technology Division are less likely to be embraced, more likely to generate friction, and ultimately may disempower future dialogue on engagements beyond CRM. An effective governance structure is a great mechanism to facilitate improved alignment. In scenarios where business proposals will—if implemented—yield poor technical outcomes (which, viewed through a certain lens, is a poor business outcome), CRM expert Tim Kippley of Rightpoint Consulting in Chicago described the process of engagement to evaluate the process–technology alignment challenge:

It's a bit of a dance. If you can get a compromise, that's the best outcome. You don't necessarily want to bend the system so far to achieve a goal. Even if you can weigh it in terms of what it will cost to build and maintain, is it really worth it, or can we find a middle ground? Or we can come up with some alternate ways. Maybe it does result in a technology customization but less customization than was originally proposed and also a slight change to the business process. It's a compromise. Nobody gets 100% of what they want. It could be a little bit of a bend on the business side along with not too much on the IT side—hopefully not to the point where you're ripping up the system to build a new feature.[2]

Given what appears to be a growing propensity of organizations to engage in aggressive customization, it is surprising that so few firms are truly evaluating a build versus buy decision. Packaged software has positioned itself as a cost saver while promising to be easily customizable. Firms may not actually be saving money, however, if they purchase a packaged product and tear it open and retool it from the ground up. During a 2016 interview, another leading CRM consultant noted the following observations gleaned from his or her long tenure in the field:

> Modern CRM apps are very flexible. They are more structured in certain ways, but they do enable you to bolt-on customizations. A lot of times clients select CRM that off the shelf has a lot of built-in modules and they proceed to twist it so it doesn't resemble the application that they purchased. At that point, I wonder: why didn't you just build your own system? You're so far off from the CRM as you purchased it. If a specialist in this application comes in, they're not going to know what to do with it, because you've customized it so much, effectively undermined the reasoning that led you to choose a packaged solution in the first place.
>
> Leverage the application for what it provides. Don't go off and customize it so much that you lose out on the benefits of future releases and future functionality. You made a decision to implement a packaged CRM software. You made the decision not to build your own. Stick with that decision. And leverage all of the benefits that come with packaged CRM software.[3]

System Controls and Process Discipline

One of the purported benefits of using any standardized software is the ability to enforce process discipline by using system controls. In 2010, Strong and Volkoff observed that enforcing this process discipline led to decreased efficiency by "increasing the interdependence among tasks that, in the legacy systems, had been loosely coupled and so relatively independent."[1] There is undoubtedly a trade-off to be considered here. While one could argue that data quality would be improved in scenarios where one system became the single point of entry, this comes at the expense of process efficiency. We should consider not only whether every step in our process should be required but also whether or not our system is handling task assignments effectively. In the example we noted above, the enterprise system required users "to perform some tasks in sequence, rather than in parallel, lengthening the time required for process completion."[1] The responsibility remains with organizations and their implementation partners to evaluate the magnitude of operational efficiency, which will be lost in favor of tighter data input controls. As we will see later during our discussion of big data, the impulse exists now more than ever to cram extensive data points into a CRM in hopes of gleaning profound customer insights, even when no evidence exists that these data points can be used to realize results or predict future behaviors and buying patterns. The research we have explored here provides insight into the reality that this approach may have significant operational consequences.

Adoption Risks—Explicit and Implied

Business units do not always—understandably—recognize the breadth of impact from customization, which includes increased maintenance costs, training implications, and decreased usage. It would not be inconceivable that CRM training curriculum could rapidly expand to the point of taking many hours, leaving firms with the decision: bolster training resources or deliver incomplete, subpar training. Firms could benefit from educating end users on the drawbacks of customization, which they would feel on a day-to-day basis. One of the most critical to users is the risk of degraded system performance and response times. Another is demonstrating the complexity of various screens. Particularly, those screens which will be accessed regularly, a visual of the results of extensive customization may give users pause and encourage them to engage in a dialogue about business processes and opportunities to improve them.

Another risk to user adoption is the reactive position in which packaged products place organizations in the context of required upgrades—a position even less desirable in the context of extensive customizations. If firms have not prepared their resourcing allocation to accommodate these challenges, they will find themselves scrambling to do so in a less organized fashion. If your firm does plan for such changes, a packaged product does have the potential to keep your IT environment current, given that you have no choice but to keep pace. Even if the vendor upgrade is a true upgrade—which is not always the case—end users will question the necessity of the change. They may not understand or care about the underlying technology

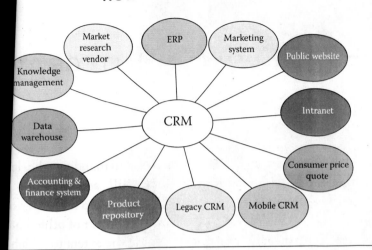

11.1   CRM integration possibilities.

m. Such integrations, as the authors went on to note, influence
mer satisfaction as a result of the integration's ability to influence
marketing capabilities and also through increased operational
ency. Using CRM as a system of record for customer data, for
ple, and piping that data into ERP or other systems eliminate
ndancy and risk of inconsistencies in customer data across
forms.

ome of the extant literature about integrations points to the impor-
e of resourcing, which underscores the notion that IT personnel,
articular, focus on CRM and potentially integrated systems, cau-
ing firms to remember that "if the IT system is not comprised of
nted workers that are flexible and able to work in other depart-
nts, the CRM system will not work and that flexibility is the key to
RM integration because of the changing environment, IT platforms
d independence of data models."[3] Once again, we see the impor-
ce of employee alignment. Only when effective employee align-
ent is achieved—employees across business and technical units able
speak the same language and relate to one another's challenges—
n integrations truly succeed.

To further increase the appeal of integrations, Liu, Liu, and Xu's
013) study included a conclusion, the impacts of which will echo
practitioners continue to make decisions surrounding their tech-
ology landscape. The study suggested that the successful integra-
on of ERP and CRM points to "the importance of broader IT

drivers to the decision, but they will grumble about the change and
if it is actually a downgrade from existing functionality and usability,
your vendor will have effectively undercut your entire CRM adoption
effort.

Reduced Technical Agility and Ability to Educate Users

We have discussed increased financial and human capital costs to customized solutions. Of particular import, however, to business users
is the impact of the overhead required to maintain customizations.
When business units request features in the future, resources that
could have been spent on implementing those requests are to some
degree already allocated to maintain customizations, decreasing from
the overall IT resource pool. The more customizations required, the
greater the ongoing resource commitment must be to maintaining,
troubleshooting, and updating the system. Unchecked customizations
also increase the resources required to maintain the extended knowledge management repository. During our discussion of business–IT
alignment, we noted the potential paradox that may exist when processes are coupled too tightly to technology and one source of this
paradox is certainly the administrative overhead required by either
consultants or internal IT on an ongoing basis to maintain, enhance,
and ensure customizations are compatible with future upgrades.

After many years of unchecked customization, many systems will
become slow and too nebulous to lend themselves to effective user
education. As new folks join the organization, the sheer volume of
overhead—coupled with, for example, poor system performance—
will almost guarantee these new users will not become CRM adopters.
This becomes a dual-faceted frustration for firms who have spent years
pouring resources into expanding their CRM and making it more
aligned to their business processes—with all the best intentions—
only to find that one day the CRM has become a monster, which actually is taking value from the organization rather than adding value.
Now, these organizations find themselves staring down the barrel of a
large capital expenditure on top of all the resources already spent. As
Rightpoint Consulting's cofounder, Brad Schneider, noted elsewhere
in this book, a lot of CRM projects occur in the reimplementation
space.

Chapter Summary

In summary, it is useful for business managers to understand the long-term implications of packaged software customizations and how customizing beyond a certain point will cause diminished ongoing return on IT investment and decreased ability to keep pace with future feature requests. As we explored in Chapter 4 on alignment, business units will need to partner with Technology to engage in a two-way dialogue. It is imperative that an organizational culture exists where Technology has the management support to vocalize concerns about specific business requests and partner with business units to develop compromises that do not degrade the quality of the system. In some cases, such compromises may even result in improved business processes, supporting our discussion that quality technology may effect changes that will ultimately be welcomed by the business.

References

1. Strong, D. M., & Volkoff, O. (2010, December). Understanding organization-enterprise system fit: A path to theorizing the information technology artifact. *MIS Quarterly 34(4)*, 731–756.
2. Kippley, T., & Schneider, B. (2016, February 18). CRM practitioners—Rightpoint (S. J. Kinnett, Interviewer).
3. Anonymous. (2016, January 12–13). Making CRM successful—CRM practitioner interview (S. J. Kinnett, Interviewer).

Just as firms must make key decisions configuration and customization they w customer relationship management (CRM) consensus surrounding CRM's role in the c systems. In particular, firms need to decide t will be integrated with other systems, taki benefits and challenges that come with pur We will see that integration decisions are cl surrounding customization or configuration. with another system could minimize the nee ization. For many firms, integrating CRM w present a number of benefits. A 2012 study o S. Dong concluded that firms should "augme CRM systems with internal systems and from tems to enhance information flow."[1] Other essa principle, including a 2013 study by Liu, Liu, an "CRM applications create value mainly through

This observation underscores the reality that C way from its roots in sales force automation and is pensable component of organizations' focus and One of the most popular and potentially rewarding occurs between CRM and an enterprise resource p tems but the landscape for potential integrations ha Even as CRM platforms enhance their native capa bolt-on packages, the following diagram shows exa systems, which could benefit from integration with C

Liu, Liu, and Xu's (2013) study noted above sug just the ingestion of information from other system yields benefits but also the exporting of customer r mation from CRM into other enterprise systems s infrastructure integration, instead of cumulating functional modules within a software system."[2] This conclusion is of particular relevance as many CRM platforms expand their capabilities to include, for example, billing. Future research comparing the outcomes of firms using integrations in favor of the expansion of CRM functionality via additional models will be of use as firms look to make strategic decisions.

Contextual Factors: Market Differentiation

While the literature clearly shows a number of general benefits, some of the CRM literature has shown that not all integrations bring equal levels of benefit. For example, for firms competing in markets with higher product differentiation or lower barriers to entry, CRM–ERP integration is more critical than in markets with high barriers to entry or low market differentiation. If your firm faces high barriers to market entry or low product differentiation, extra consideration should be taken before deciding to integrate CRM with ERP. In fact, given the high overhead, complexity, cost, and time required to integrate systems, we recommend firms to first examine the quality of their CRM system as an autonomous unit. The quality of existing integrations should also be examined, with the aim being to ensure both CRM and its integrated systems are collectively satisfying the design hierarchy of needs (discussed in the next chapter). This is also an opportunity to conduct larger analysis on existing business processes. Finally, after thinking through these considerations, firms could look to identify specific, strategic integration points.

Understanding Risks and Alternatives

For all the potential benefits that integration with CRM can bring to an organization, a leading industry CRM consultant called out integrations as the most difficult facets of CRM implementation, highlighting them as an area in which unrealistic resource estimates or insufficient planning may have catastrophic consequences. The consultant's exact comments are as follows:

> Integrations [are the most difficult aspect of CRM]. Integration with other systems, integrations with ERP. Sometimes they go so smoothly.

But when you're integrating with legacy applications from 20 years ago, when you don't have the option to upgrade that software as well, it makes things very difficult. You start to get into back-building things to work with a modern CRM application. [Organizations] often don't understand the implications of launching CRM in terms of how other systems are going to work with the CRM. They may jump to conclusions about what CRM can do for their end users and they forget there are a lot of backend systems feeding CRM. So I would say they don't resource enough team members to work on their other systems. CRM is not natively a heavyweight structure to build. It's the data and other systems that serve it that can become very heavy.[4]

This suggests taking extra time, going the extra mile, convening that extra meeting to ensure integration details are fully understood may be more critical than in many other areas. To that end, consider a scenario where a CRM upgrade is requested by sales and accommodated by management. The finance and accounting system, however, was integrated into the previous CRM solution and that integration would need to be rebuilt with the new CRM. Based on our consultant's insights above, the organization might actually benefit from upgrading its finance system concurrently and providing a single cutover. It would not be unreasonable if the challenge and cost of integration from a legacy finance system to a modern CRM could outweigh or at least rival corresponding challenges and costs of upgrading the finance system and integrating it to the new CRM.

An aged but relevant study conducted by Ron Miller in 2007 noted that inferior integration initiatives result when firms focus on more of a "point-to-point solution to move a specific type of information from one system to another, rather than a comprehensive way of sharing information across the two systems."[5] His comments should not be misconstrued as a prescription for voluminous integration, but rather they represent an insight about the lens through which organizations may view the decision-making process as to whether to use an additional module to an existing system rather than a full integration. If the integration solution is point to point and cannot be positioned— as Miller noted—as a comprehensive way to share information across the systems, this may be an indication that an existing system enhancement may be a more prudent course of action. This would be especially true if the resourcing of the team supporting the system to be integrated with CRM is not well staffed.

Content and Knowledge Management Systems

Aside from ERP, another popular integration that has received attention in the extant literature is the integration between enterprise content management—sometimes referred to as knowledge management—systems and CRM. In this section, we will evaluate opportunities for content management (CM) integration and highlight some of the fundamental principles behind successful CM. Miller's 2007 essay noted that CRM and CM systems differ in the way they relate to data, namely, that "CRM collects structured data about customers and sales, while [CM], for the most part, organizes unstructured documents."[5] In 2007, CM systems may have been a slightly advanced mechanism of collecting documents in one place, but it has evolved to include both structured and unstructured data. To that end, the modern CMS has plenty of opportunities for structure, including but not limited to most systems' ability to create custom lists, define and enforce workflows, and allow for customization of required fields to improve the robust nature of CM and improve system structure.

One example of a simple but useful integration is a CRM-housed search of the CM repository on customer name and organization name. This is a slick way to determine whether customers (or prospects) have been referenced in other proposals or marketing collateral. It may be enough to answer the question: are there touchpoints with my clients that are occurring outside the CRM, which are stored in unstructured content? Extending this point, suppose we are inheriting a legacy CRM, which suffered from a poor data conversion from a prior system, or suffered from poor adoption, or came after the implementation of your CMS and no back engineering was in scope for that project. Adding a basic search bar to a contact detail screen provides a simple mechanism to leverage core CMS functionality without the need for significant retraining or change management initiatives. This comes at the comparatively minor technical cost of sending a search string to the CM system's application programming interface (API). The search and its results occur wholly within the CMS. We do not want to pervert a CRM with something it is not or should not be; we want to enhance, enrich, and empower it. From a tactical perspective, Miller suggests companies "use middleware applications; partner with other vendors; hire consultants; or use programming techniques such as simple object access protocol (SOAP), web services, and service-oriented architecture (SOA) as ways to get the two systems to communicate."[5]

Chapter Summary

In this chapter, we have explored the vast landscape of integrations available to CRM. We understand that the literature has highlighted particular benefit from integration of CRM with ERP systems as well as CRM with enterprise content management systems. The decision to integrate CRM should be influenced by honest resource assessments, keeping in mind that integrations have been noted to be the most difficult aspect of implementing CRM and that lack of effective personnel resourcing can have detrimental consequences.

Given the number of integration options available, firms can benefit from prioritization exercises as they seek to understand exactly which systems can most benefit from customer relationship data and which systems can conversely contribute tangible benefit to CRM without introducing unnecessary clutter (a real risk). While ERP and CMS have received particular attention in the literature highlighted in this chapter, let us not interpret it as prescriptive. Every firm's unique needs—as understood through introspection and cross-functional collaboration—will dictate the value it receive from integration and if the challenge, costs, and nature of the potential systems to be integrated will be outweighed by the benefits.

References

1. Dong, S. (2012). Decision execution mechanisms of IT governance: The CRM case. *International Journal of Information Management 32*, 147–157.
2. Liu, A. Z., Liu, H., & Xu, S. X. (2013). How do competitive environments moderate CRM value? *Decision Support Systems 56*, 462–473.

3. Elmuti, D., Jia, H., & Gray, D. (2009). Customer relationship management strategic application and organizational effectiveness: An empirical investigation. *Journal of Strategic Marketing 17(1)*, 75–96.
4. Anonymous. (2016). Making CRM successful—CRM practitioner interview. (S. J. Kinnett, Interviewer).
5. Miller, R. (2007). The courtship of CRM and CM. *EContent 30*, 40–43.

12
KEEPING THE MIND IN MIND

It is not a coincidence that a significant portion of this book is devoted to highlighting the importance of interaction design and software quality. These are not only two generally relevant topics but they are also glaringly absent from most existing customer relationship management (CRM) models. When we speak of interaction design, this is a term roughly synonymous with human–computer interaction (HCI), a discipline that draws knowledge from a number of various fields of study, including cognitive psychology and sociology, and applies this knowledge to advance the cause of computing. According to a 2012 essay by Uday Gajendar, HCI practitioners in this field seek "to identify, understand, and quantify the human factor in computing."[1] The discipline prides itself on being formalized, delivering quantifiable data, and identifying repeatable activities. These activities and processes provide schemas through which HCI practitioners can shape future projects. We posit that diligent, consistent focus on HCI principles is a significant differentiator between firms that achieve CRM success and those that do not.

Research has shown that the more users of the system need to think, the less likely they will be able to develop a repeatable work pattern to increase their efficiency. Lidwell, Holden, and Butler's 2010 book *Universal Principles of Design* informs us that a human's range of cognitive abilities is narrow compared to perceptual abilities and, as a result, "it is generally easier to design activities and environments that achieve immersion through perceptual stimulation than through cognitive engagement."[2] In other words, CRM should be as cognitively unstimulating as possible and provide perceptual stimulation through its design and responsiveness. There is certainly support for the idea of embracing more graphics within CRM, an approach that could facilitate perceptual stimulation. Some CRM systems are implemented with pages so packed with fields and lists, the amount of system training, technical acumen, and functional knowledge required to learn—let alone master—the system is staggering. We recognize that hosted packaged software solutions have limited options when it comes to graphics. Thin-client (server-driven) applications are currently constrained, generally, in what they can deliver compared to thick-client (client-side) applications. Firms can benefit from understanding that thin-client solutions have limitations with real impacts and should be weighed in the analysis process.

Design Hierarchy of Needs

In order to understand what is important to users to feel comfortable using a system, we will draw parallels to basic human psychology. Extending the points made above, Lidwell, Holden, and Butler defined a hierarchy of needs analogous to Maslow's hierarchy, which proposes peoples' needs are ordered in importance, and one's achievement of a particular need serves as a prerequisite to achieving higher levels. Maslow's hierarchy is from lower level to higher level:

1. Physiological needs
2. Safety
3. Love
4. Self-esteem
5. Self-actualization

The design hierarchy of needs which we will use as a framework for our discussion is as follows (Figure 12.1):

1. Functionality
2. Reliability
3. Usability

Figure 12.1   Design hierarchy of needs chart.

4. Proficiency
5. Creativity

Experience has shown that the vast majority of CRMs fail to meet the second and third tiers—reliability and usability—of this hierarchy. Functionality is usually taken care of because the current standard is to cram as much as possible into a CRM with the speculation that it will be measured, eventually. Interestingly, it is the overfocus on functionality which results in the failure of reliability. Especially, in the case of packaged software, extensive customizations are breeding grounds for creating gaps in reliability for the sake of functionality. Rarely, do we hear of a firm scaling back CRM functionality. It is always expanding as the pet projects of many managers continuing to multiply.

Functionality

Functionality is the base level of the hierarchy. When we think about functionality in this context, we are talking about the basic ability of a system to perform the tasks for which it was built. Whether it executes these tasks effectively or consistently is a matter for evaluation at the next two levels of the design hierarchy. Given one of our core assertions—beauty in simplicity—we must draw the distinction between streamlining various CRM functions while retaining those which are necessary such as—which we would typically consider in the CRM case to be—sales force automation tools such as contact management and basic opportunity tracking.

Reliability

If CRM—or any system—is to be successful, it must be reliable. Recall from our chapter on positioning the Technology Division that the division can be evaluated as being at one of three points of the technology maturity model: competency, credibility, or commitment. The core level, competency, is directly correlated to the reliability of the CRM system. Nothing screams IT incompetency like application bugs. Unhandled exceptions, server time-outs, and disappearing or freezing screens are all priority 1 for CRM practitioners. For the business stakeholder, this means lobbying for these types of issues to be corrected as a priority. For the IT professional, this means coming to an understanding that these items are even more important than the shiny projects being tossed around in senior management meetings.

Some experience has shown that convincing the business to delay whatever pet project an executive dreamed up waiting in the dentist's office for the sake of providing a more reliable system can be difficult. One of the most effective mechanisms we have seen to achieve this goal is facilitating the means for stakeholders to *see* these problems in action. As CRM stakeholders observe their sales force bashing their heads against the wall as they experience workflow disruptions and instability, they will be more likely to prioritize fixes to infrastructure and reliability. Seeing is believing.

It can be tempting to handle bugs as isolated production support items, an incomplete tactic which breeds workarounds in lieu of solutions: quick fixes which work for a particular contact record, for example, but do not extend in the direction of systematic strategies. As part of any IT support tracking system, it is critical to identify trends in any application bugs that are reported and to schedule patch releases on a regular basis. If you are using a hosted solution, ensure that your contract has ample allowances for robust system support and commitments to reliability and timely error handling.

Usability

The majority of our discussion will be about Tier 3: Usability, which Rogers, Sharp, and Preece in 2011 defined as the act of "ensuring that interactive products are easy to learn, effective to use, and enjoyable from the user's perspective."[3] Firms must begin to treat their enterprise software applications the same way that consumer-facing software views itself with an ongoing focus being placed on accessibility, usability, and adoption. Before we dive too deeply into design particulars, we need to acknowledge that what might seem like the little things—for example: color, button placement, and font choices—are in fact key contributors to user adoption. The design must be visually pleasing if we are to realize the benefits of the *aesthetic-usability effect*, which is defined as "a phenomenon in which people perceive more aesthetic designs as easier to use than less aesthetic designs—whether they are or not."[2] We may note here the parallel to the technology acceptance model (TAM) which states that perceived ease of use (PEOU) influences perceived usefulness which subsequently influences behavioral intent to use the system. Bringing these concepts together shows us that understanding and harnessing the aesthetic-usability effect bolsters the potential to achieve PEOU and all the subsequent benefits it provides.

Princely Ifinedo brought together the relationship between TAM and the aesthetic-usability effect in a 2011 study where he concluded that "where the technical attributes of an IT application are perceived to be high, its semantic features tend to be assessed likewise."[4] Aesthetic designs help people feel more comfortable using a CRM and will increase usage and adoption. Cluttered, ugly CRMs will result in negative user-to-system relationships, which result in narrowed thinking and stifled creativity. Stressful environments—essentially every corporate environment today—and multitasking increase fatigue and reduce cognitive performance, making our challenge even more difficult and important to overcome.

Errors   Effective error handling, both on the user and back-end sides of the equation, is important to achieving usability. The design principle of *forgiveness* is of particular relevance here. As explained by Lidwell, Holden, and Butler in 2010, forgiveness suggests that software should not only help people avoid errors but also minimize the consequences of those errors if and when they present themselves. Some experience has shown that CRM systems have been notably poor in their error messages. A web interface might allow a user to complete an entire screen's worth of data for, say, contact entry. Upon clicking Save, the CRM displays a generic "complete required fields" message with crude highlighting of the field missing. Consider going the extra mile to tailor error messages to be as useful and actionable as possible. We want to strive for messages which are courteous, avoid condemnation, and provide clear direction on how to remedy the issue and move forward.

Proficiency

We touched briefly upon stress and some of the challenges it presents. In particular, the inverse relationship between usability and stress feeds aptly into the concept of proficiency, the fourth level of the hierarchy. Lidwell et al. explained that proficiency is all about empowering users to do things better than they might have in the past. Further, users have been shown to perceive proficient designs as high value. When usability fails, the system becomes burdensome: the semantic opposite of proficiency. Ultimately, a usable system is a necessary but not sufficient precursor to proficiency. Users must still be well educated in business processes and intricacies of the system. It would typically take a strong training program including continuing education in CRM to yield these benefits fully.

Creativity

The final level of the hierarchy, creativity, is only possible when the prior levels of the hierarchy have been fulfilled. At this level, users may develop cult-like followings and become natural evangelists of the system resulting largely from their satisfaction with the system's design, which enables users' creativity. Management would presumably value creative use of CRM systems and advocate for such use by their employees, perhaps even setting expectations that users engage systems at the creative level. At the same time, management may neglect the first four preconditions, resulting in unreasonable expectations and breeding user resentment. Examples of using a CRM system creatively would be to use flexible functionality to achieve a personalized goal which is not built into core functionality, such as a personalized method of contact tagging and segmentation. Analytical CRM also provides opportunities for creativity-given analytical CRM's potential to identify client trends and—in some cases—predict future behaviors.

Hick's Law

One of the most important design principles with regard to implementing an effective CRM system is Hick's law, which states "that the time required to make a decision is a function of the number of available options."[2] Firms may gain efficiencies by reducing numbers of required fields but may gain even more advantage by eliminating those fields altogether. A strong mechanism to ensure success in this area is to begin with a given number of unrequired fields and run a basic report every quarter to see which of the optional fields users populate of their own accord. Over time, this exercise will show opportunities to reduce fields, improve screen real estate, and even uncover opportunities for new fields which could replace those deemed useless. As with all areas of CRM, if you cannot point to a singular benefit from tracking and reporting on any given field and the salespeople do not need it, get rid of it. Over time, initiatives to remove fields from CRM systems will become as important—if not more important—as so-called enhancements.

Performance Load and Required Fields

Hick's law is of great use to us as we evaluate which fields we should be including within our CRM screens. In my experience, many CRM systems are bloated not only with too many choices for various picklists (drop-downs) but also too many total required fields (and fields in general). Picklists, being so easy to configure, become bloated perhaps the most quickly especially when coupled with what are often called dependent picklists: picklists that become relevant and present customized choices depending on decisions made when populating the primary picklist. In our chapter on system support, we will examine the bloated picklist phenomenon in one of its most common contexts: support tickets. Poor decisions in this context will, as we will see, alienate both users and IT personnel, making bloated picklists especially foolish to implement.

Returning to required fields, considering natural reluctance to do more than is necessary, we find ourselves falling victim to a concept called performance load, which states, "the greater the effort to accomplish a task, the less likely the task will be accomplished successfully."[2] Reducing the number of required fields in your CRM streamlines data entry and modification and improves code efficiency. Apply Hick's law to every configurable field in your CRM system and watch as your data become more clear, robust, and actionable.

Data Quality Reduction

A 2010 study by Strong and Volkoff of an enterprise software implementation highlighted the danger of using required fields inappropriately. The study found that the system's data capture mechanisms were ineffective with regard to placing an order within the system. The new system demanded that repair orders be priced at the beginning of the order entry process, but the true, accurate price could not be known until the level of effort for the job was quantified, a process that occurred only after repairs had begun. This example is emblematic of a key principle: *required fields should not be involved in situations where the accurate selection of said field is not immediately possible.*

Consider a scenario where our principal audience—salespeople— not only have a required field present at a time when they cannot populate it with an informed decision but also see no personal value to the field as a contribution to their own prospecting activities. Further, if they have not bought-in to the value of the data to management, it is very difficult to imagine any positive outcomes unless, on the off chance, the new data points yield some sort of eureka moment from an analytics perspective. To that end, adding required fields *feels* like it would improve data quality. After all, you have guaranteed another data input, which will increase the analytics engine ability to provide insights. Our discussion of analytics explores this classic misconception.

A related and perhaps more prevalent issue occurs as a result of the best of intentions. For example, consider that, upon creation of an Opportunity record, the system utilizes uniform naming conventions to name the Opportunity. Such functionality could concatenate a few key opportunity fields to create consistent nomenclature. While this may be extremely beneficial, in the event that the name creation logic only occurs when the Opportunity record is saved, but the opportunity name is required upon Opportunity creation, we find ourselves in a situation where a user's naming decision is overwritten by the automatic name creation.

This generates confusion. Over time, the user will become used to this and populate the Opportunity Name field with gibberish, whatever is easy. This practice may bleed into other data entry areas. If the user did put thought into the naming of the Opportunity, only to see that thought deemed to be irrelevant as a result of the automatic naming, the user will experience frustration. This example is a classic imposition misfit. As we discussed in our chapter on customization, impositions are the result of inherent characteristics in the system such as, in this example, the required Opportunity Name field. Something should not be present when you are not able to appropriately act on it. Recall that impositions are considered more serious than the other type of misfit: deficiencies.

Transaction Inefficiencies

Required fields increase the time it takes to complete a given transaction within the CRM system which will, over time and as more and more required fields are added, result in a very real frustration from end users. After all the effort placed into adoption, firms can easily undo a large portion of their gains by making common transactions—entering phone calls, for example—more difficult to complete. As with the "add another checkbox" mentality, fields can be set as required in mere minutes, if not less, and management is all too aware of that reality.

Presentation and Optics

Research in HCI points to the importance of decisions around presentation and optics as having real results on a user's ability to thrive using a piece of software. Packaged software may provide limited options for individual presentation decisions. Systems can be configured extensively, but the actual graphical overlay may be out of a practitioner's control. One area where flexibility might exist is in the presentation of text. In such cases where flexibility does exist, Lidwell, Holden, and Butler suggest in their 2010 book on design that—when it comes to making decisions about text presentation—"bolding is generally preferred over [italics or underlining] as it adds minimal noise to the design and clearly highlights target elements."[2] They note that italics, while not as noisy, are harder to see and less legible. They further suggest underlining is the noisiest presentation approach and should be avoided.

In the case of packaged software, or software developed such that it would make use of Web standards such as blue, underlined hyperlinks, we may need to balance ideal highlighting principles with existing realities, thereby achieving consistency, a principle stating that "systems are more usable and learnable when similar parts are expressed in similar ways."[2] While, in this example, we favor bolding, we would not recommend making a hyperlink bold and omitting the standard underline, as it becomes counterintuitive to the user that the hyperlink is actually a hyperlink. In the user's mind, the CRM is, in this example, just another application he or she accesses through an Internet browser and the principles he or she has observed and found to be consistent in general should be true within the CRM in particular.

Progressive Disclosure

The principle of progressive disclosure, defined as "a strategy for managing information complexity in which only necessary or requested information is displayed at any given time" (p. 188),[2] may well be considered a contrarian approach to designing effective solutions. In particular, progressive disclosure is one of the most compelling arguments against click counts as the end-all, be all, measurement of usability, which it has clearly become as of the writing of this book. Partly driven by the structure and out of the box presentation capabilities of many packaged CRM products, practitioners can—again, driven in no small measure by mandates to reduce click counts—look to provide every possible piece of information about an object on a single page, no matter how much scrolling may be required. Hovering functionality is an example of a feature in many packaged CRM products, which seeks to hide information until it was needed. No doubt the designers had the best of intentions, but we would posit many users would agree, however, that accidentally moving the mouse over a piece of data that generates a hover is among one of the most frustrating aspects of interacting with a packaged CRM product.

Progressive disclosure is useful when we need to guide users through a particular process where each step of the process does not necessarily require previous steps in the process to remain front and center. In scenarios, however, where all necessary information is available at once and data points have direct, relevant relationships to one another, we may find progressive disclosure to be a hindrance. Underscoring this point is a sentiment captured in Strong and Volkoff's 2010 study of enterprise resource planning (ERP) implementation, which we treated thoroughly in a prior chapter. When one interviewee began to use the new ERP system, he expressed frustration that he knows all the necessary data for him to perform his job functions in the system, but he does not always know how to find it. In the words of another interviewee, "Now you have to go hunt.... It [used to be] exposed more. You [could] see all this information on what I call a sheet. Where in today's environment you need to screen hop."[5] Part of this sentiment could be driven simply by the user's need to adjust to the new system. Perhaps the progressive disclosure approach is appropriate but just different. Ultimately, we present progressive disclosure for consideration as evidence that, in scenarios requiring many steps and dealing with complicated information, practitioners may find embracing progressive disclosure provides simpler, more usable screens, which can be more easily adopted by the user base.

Constraint and Role Typing

Earlier in the chapter, we explored Hick's law and its importance in reducing the number of options given to users with regard to specific fields; we now turn to another key design concept: *constraint*. Lidwell, Holden, and Butler define constraint as "a method of limiting the actions that can be performed on a system."[2] One mechanism to facilitate this key design goal is through role typing—that is, identifying a set of user roles and tailoring screen design and functionality to meet those roles. For example, roles could be put in place to display or hide functionality based on the following user types:

- Marketing
- Sales support
- Frontline sales
- Management
- Administrators
- Technology

For example, the marketing function typically is responsible for the creation of marketing campaign records within the CRM. Users of role type equal to marketing would have the campaign creation functionality exposed to them, while other types—except administrators and technologists—would not see the functionality. When considering the role of constraint in the design of our CRM, we should weigh the benefits of the functionality-constrained CRM and the impact of role typing and implementation on system performance and code complexity. We must also ensure our typing exercises are robust and maintained in the event that responsibilities change. Ideally, our CRM should allow the CRM support team to add and define roles via a graphical user interface (GUI) to reduce support load on Technology.

Many packaged software products have included custom page presentation as an integral part of their core functionality, with varying levels of difficulty to implement and keep layouts nimble to accommodate ongoing business requests. The related paradigm that sometimes gets overlooked is the restriction of functionality discussed above. It is certainly true that we have advised against over-architecture, as it increases the amount of overhead placed on system administrators and makes knowledge transfer more difficult as IT personnel join and leave firms. Both things are true—we need to embrace Hick's law and the recommendations resulting from an understanding of level of exposure should be equally considered. Ultimately, firms must find their own balance. Striking this balance would be an important area to ask for guidance from CRM implementation experts.

The Inverted Pyramid

An inverted pyramid represents a structure of information presentation where the most important information is presented first; then, subsequent information is presented in progressively less important order. In an inverted pyramid, the least important piece of information is presented last. Inverted pyramid structures are appropriate when ordering the values in picklists as well as when choosing field layouts on a screen. Alphabetical or numerically ascending or descending models of presentation are often used and practitioners may, in some cases, conclude such approaches are best, but in the context of items with absolute priority relative to each other, consider leveraging the inverted pyramid construct. Recall that we want our CRM to be as cognitively unstimulating as possible. As firms evaluate the way in which they present data in various areas of the CRM system, they should be mindful of scenarios where the inverted pyramid will yield a superior method of presentation and aid users in achieving a sense of flow: performing functions by instinct and moving throughout the CRM system effortlessly.

Chapter Summary

In this chapter, we have explored theoretical design foundations and principles and their implications on CRM implementations. Understanding the design hierarchy of needs will provide important insights into the ways that our implementation decisions influence psychological factors, which in turn influence the way users interact with and ultimately whether they choose to adopt the system. Additionally, we have explored design concepts including Hick's law, constraint, and the inverted pyramid, which, when embraced, all provide the potential to make real impacts on usability. These principles provide theoretical foundations to capabilities now present in most packaged CRM products. Finally, we have challenged conventional wisdom surrounding click counts by presenting the concept of progressive disclosure, providing a counterargument to embracing the click count reduction mandate myopically.

References

1. Gajendar, U. (2012, May and June). Finding the sweet spot of design. *Interactions 19(3)*, 10–11.
2. Lidwell, W., Holden, K., & Butler, J. (2010). *Universal Principles of Design*. Beverly, MA: Rockport.
3. Rogers, Y., Sharp, H., & Preece, J. (2011). *Interaction Design: Beyond Human-Computer Interaction*. West Sussex, UK: John Wiley & Sons.
4. Ifinedo, P. (2011). Examining the influences of external expertise and in-house computer/IT knowledge on ERP system success. *The Journal of Systems and Software 84*, 2065–2078. 2074.
5. Strong, D. M., & Volkoff, O. (2010, December). Understanding organization-enterprise system fit: A path to theorizing the information technology artifact. *MIS Quarterly 34(4)*, 731–756.

13

UNDERSTANDING USER INVOLVEMENT

In Chapter 9, we examined the importance of the business analysis function with a particular focus on business requirements. We understand that requirements capture is one—arguably the most critical—but nevertheless only one component of the overall software development life cycle. We have examined mechanisms to engage users during the business analysis process. In this chapter, we will take a deeper dive into user involvement not only in the requirements process but throughout the entire customer relationship management (CRM) implementation. To begin with, user participation is an opportunity not only to ensure the requirements process is effective at capturing the needs of the business but also to set expectations and instill a sense of ownership surrounding the project.

While management of expectations is a common and often-taught skill, it is imperative when implementing CRM that users experience as few surprises as possible when the system goes live. We have explored user resistance and cynicism at length. Failing to manage expectations during all stages of the life cycle creates a ripe breeding ground for resistance. Users will feel cheated and their discontent will spread rapidly among their colleagues. Since, especially in larger, more complicated projects, it is unlikely everything will be in perfect working order when it is time to take the system live, even difficult decisions made at the 11th hour must be transparent to users.

We now understand the importance of user involvement throughout the CRM implementation process. The challenge, however, with involving users in the actual design of the system is in determining the extent users will be involved. As we have explored in the design section about users versus experts driving results, users have important contributions but they should not be conflated with CRM or design experts. What seems like the right choice offhand in a meeting may not pass the test of time, which of course is one reason why iterative development has become so popular. The nature of packaged software suggests that users would not necessarily have much influence on software design itself, but they can contribute to workflow methods or configuration decisions. Users may come to the table with the assumption that the system can do anything, and indeed some practitioners embrace this sentiment and deploy customizations without hesitation. As a result of these user perceptions, project architects will need to be constantly on guard that users are communicating their needs from a business perspective but not prescribing specific technology solutions. Especially as consumer technology gains adoption by greater segments of the population, increased technical literacy has the potential to create would-be experts especially eager to share their newfound expertise.

Paradoxically, tech-savvy users can actually inhibit progress as they may be more likely to complicate solutions because of their greater knowledge of the breadth of options available. In the case of CRM software, we do essentially want to design for the lowest common denominator—at least for initial releases—so basic wins. Some tech-savvy users understand this and may have more creative solutions. The key is to keep an ear to the ground of user participation. If you identify a tech-savvy user begin to dominate design conversations and propose ideas not easily grasped by the less technically oriented users, it may be time to have a conversation or to adopt a more authoritative design process. A more authoritative design process would present users with a small number of potential designs, created by the user experience architect and the group would discuss and arrive at a consensus. A relevant caution against carte blanche user focus comes from Uday Gajendar. Writing on the topics of interface design and human–computer interaction in a 2012 essay, he noted that "an exclusive focus on users seems unwise. Users, after all, can be messy, complicated, inarticulate, self-contradictory and emotional."[1] His sentiments about the specific interface design process are just as applicable to the design and configuration of CRM systems.

A separate but related consideration surrounds process improvement. While users may be quite good at presenting the challenges they face with the existing process or system (though there are certainly no guarantees, hence the importance of user shadowing and exhaustive requirements elicitation processes), they may be less effective when proposing solutions to these challenges. Their paradigm is likely to be very tactical as they seek to pull the proverbial thorn from the paw, which can lead to emotional postures. As Gajendar noted, above, users can exhibit a number of unsavory traits—through no fault of their own—which could cloud judgment surrounding implementation decisions. When users become prescriptive, the savvy practitioner has the opportunity to reflect the users' requests and empathize with their challenges, go away to research options, and come back to present the recommended solution. Experience has shown predominantly cases where users were overinvolved in making decisions they were not qualified to make.

Parkinson's Law of Triviality

Striking the user-involvement balance is especially important given our need to guard against the dangers of Parkinson's law of triviality, which states that when groups come together to evaluate a problem, they tend to spend most of their time on the most trivial matters. To complicate matters further, because certain users or stakeholders *perceive* themselves to be experts in technology, as we discussed, they feel empowered—perhaps even obligated—to argue about every little point upon which they have an opinion. A related corollary of the law of triviality is that the amount of chatter and discussion generated by a change is inversely proportional to the complexity of the change.

A classic example of this principle in action occurs during discussions of field layouts. Should email be above or below phone number? All users reference emails and phone numbers in their jobs; therefore they—via the phenomenon where people will be more vocal simply because they possess the ability to provide commentary—will spend disproportionate amounts of time lobbying for their various positions. Meanwhile, time that could be spent on more complex decisions, which still require user input, but that not all users may be positioned to address, is spent on field placement. It is true that field placement decisions are important but may be receiving disproportionate weighting considering the risks in the form of time, which could be better spent on other tasks. The law of triviality and its corollaries remind us to guard against overanalysis. It is more than just mere rhyme which has caused the phrase "analysis paralysis" to become ubiquitous in the corporate world. For items with more trivial impact, such as certain field layout decisions, practitioners should allot less time than they would for larger matters such as process flows or business logic.

User Acceptance Testing

Software testing is arguably one of the most arduous and most disliked aspects of any system implementation and CRM is no different. We know that users' perceptions of CRM are paramount, but during the testing process, they may identify a number of defects, souring their initial impressions of system quality. Particularly given the often-used title of "user acceptance testing" (UAT), users may enter testing with a perception that everything should be perfect and they will walk out at the end of the day with a sense of acceptance and maybe even comfort. As CRM practitioners know, it rarely goes so smoothly. The functional testing exercise is extremely useful, but we should start calling UAT what it really is: users banging on the system trying to break it.

Business stakeholders have been known to express concerns about functional testing, demonstrating skepticism surrounding issues including the time requirement, necessity ("Why can't the consultants do it?"), and the risk of poor perception outcomes. Some of these concerns could be mitigated by the repositioning of what testing is: not necessarily a time to gain comfort and acceptance of the system, but an exercise in testing system accuracy and reliability. The resistance to allocating users' time and energy by pulling them into testing exercises and away from other responsibilities is equally pertinent to the project team. At this stage in the project, we can presume they are already running on fumes and desperately need time to resolve outstanding defects, review deployment plans, and perform technical testing, among other tasks, and instead find themselves locked in a room creating test data [and augmenting test scripts]. At this stage, most users still require handholding and voice frustrations both about the time being asked of them as well as any issues they might encounter.

Taking all these factors together, we could benefit from creating an environment that requires minimal amount of project team member involvement to facilitate testing, set clear expectations about what the testing process is and is not, and ensure users understand that they should not expect to walk out of the sessions with mastery of the system—that comes later, through training. Gaining consensus around these points will be easier with sufficient alignment and candid dialogue ahead of time.

Chapter Summary

We have seen from the extant literature and heard from CRM experts that user involvement is an indispensable part of CRM initiatives. In this chapter, we explored factors which, if not understood and taken into account when engaging users, may yield less than desirable outcomes. Parkinson's law of triviality teaches us that users—and perhaps practitioners if they are not careful—will tend to focus on the easiest facets of developing the CRM system and tend to avoid engaging in discussion of more complicated concepts. We also examined specific considerations related to UAT, an area of CRM implementation that is necessarily heavy in user involvement, arriving at an understanding that expectations management will be critical to ensuring users walk away from testing without having their support of CRM compromised by frustrations that may arise from the testing process.

Reference

1. Gajendar, U. (2012, May & June). Finding the sweet spot of design. *Interactions 19*, 10–11.

PART III
MANAGEMENT

14

USER EDUCATION

In this chapter, we will explore a number of topics related to user education and training, including positioning, curriculum, and best practices. At this point in the project life cycle, both practitioners and users involved thus far are likely to be very fatigued, and it would be very easy to shortchange training initiatives, yet research and experience have shown that investing so much capital in a customer relationship management (CRM) system is rendered all but useless without an effective training program. It has become clear that not only the content of a training program, but also various environmental factors and employee perceptions about training all contribute to the success of a training initiative. We will begin by reviewing several psychological principles and mechanisms to position users to receive the greatest benefits of training.

Strengthening Users' Perceived Ability

It is not only the content of the training that enables users to acquire knowledge. The effective training initiative will also enable users to embrace technology both by providing them with tangible skills and also by empowering them with the confidence to embrace and utilize the new or enhanced software. To the latter, one way to increase user confidence is by imbibing users with a perception that the software is easy to use. Positioning the CRM system in this way will allow users to receive the training material more easily. We can see a parallel to the technology acceptance model (TAM) construct of perceived ease of use (PEOU). Recall that TAM states that PEOU influences perceived usefulness (PU), which subsequently influences users' behavioral intent—in this case, to adopt the software.

In practical terms, this could be as straightforward as using the words "easy" or "simple" throughout the training. A related cultural paradigm that positively influences training is the assumption of excellence. The cognitive structure imposed by this line of thought makes use of a known psychological phenomenon called the Pygmalion effect, which states that when people are ascribed strengths, they are more likely to behave consistently with those strengths. Both the Pygmalion effect and the Hawthorne effect (discussed in Chapter 1) are examples of the larger *expectation effect*, which is a phenomenon in which "perception and behavior changes as a result of personal expectations or the expectations of others."[1]

Users will, as a result of the expectation effect, either begin to believe that the system is easy and simple or believe that they *should* think the system is easy and simple, otherwise they lag behind their peers. This example speaks to perceived ease of use, a variable which is further strengthened by trainers who are able to move fast and know the system inside and out. This may seem obvious, but one of the key risks of user-delivered training is the possibility that users will not be proficient enough on the software to teach it to others and may stumble during classroom trainings or not be able to address on-the-fly questions.

While user-delivered training benefits from the addition of credibility and the ability to provide more complete business context to the trainings, these benefits quickly dissolve in the face of appearing unsteady on software. When salespeople train salespeople, and the trainer falters, it may have an even greater impact on the trainees. As they see a colleague—one of their own—unable to demonstrate proficiency, they may begin to believe that the software must be very difficult to use. What hope would they have of mastering it? This decreases PEOU, and consequently, TAM finds one of its variables diminished, thereby diminishing overall odds for system adoption. The lesson to firms: only commit to user-delivered training if you are also willing to invest heavily in pilot user proficiency prior to training. Despite these risks, Tim Kippley, CRM Practice Lead at Rightpoint Consulting, highlighted the appeal of user-delivered training and the usefulness of investment in the "Train the Trainer" model. Train the Trainer is a mechanism to ensure that a group of users have the confidence and ability to train their peers. In practical terms, those users involved in the implementation process become super users and subsequently have the potential to be excellent trainers. Involving users in the implementation process essentially includes the Train the Trainer concept since sufficient learning will naturally occur throughout the process to allow these users to demonstrate mastery of core knowledge. In a 2016 interview, Mr. Kippley highlighted myriad benefits of Train the Trainer, noting that clients find it

> interesting for a variety of reasons. It's very attractive cost-wise. It also starts to create champions within the organization. They're looked upon as experts. Sometimes, structurally it's like a promotion, if they've been doing a job a long time. It's a feather in their cap. "Not only am I doing xyz, I feel good about myself because I'm also the champion for our CRM." It also helps among the peer group. "Joe's using it. It can't be that bad."[2]

Overall, it is probably true that having users involved in the training process has the potential to yield greater benefits than CRM practitioner-only delivered training. For those organizations that have not involved users extensively in the implementation process, or if the included users are poor presenters or lack enthusiasm to serve as reliable system advocates, a hybrid training model should be considered. One option is to couple user-delivered training with support from a member of the implementation team or other CRM expert (such as an application support professional).

Positioning Training Initiatives Effectively

The importance of top management support—which we learned earlier is a critical predictor of CRM success or failure—appears once again in the context of training decisions. A 2010 study on training users on sales force automation noted that "management decisions about the training, including the decision to make training mandatory or not, may serve as cues about the change and the firm's commitment to the change."[3] Additional research has shown that users have demonstrated increased trust when communication is both consistent and unambiguous. This suggests sufficient prior planning to ensure that the message is clear and does not change over time. The insight from this study also underscores that top management really does need to be involved throughout the entire project life cycle in very visible ways. While we have certainly explored the importance of top management support, it remains informative to review examples of exactly what that support looks and feels like in action. We will now examine the impact of mandating training as opposed to positioning it as a voluntary exercise.

Voluntariness

While the definition of voluntariness might be straightforward—the degree to which salespeople perceive training as mandated or voluntary—it is less obvious that voluntariness is not a dichotomous decision. For example, salespeople may be told training is voluntary, but they are strongly encouraged to participate. This example betrays ambiguity on the part of management and is in conflict with the insight noted above about management's responsibility to be unambiguous in their messaging surrounding training and, as a result, will result in less effective results. The ambiguity makes it unclear just how much management values the training and believes it to be effective, which will influence users' perceptions as they evaluate whether they want to attend training and—if they do—their perceptions on efficacy.

Even in a scenario where training is optional, those users who do attend training should receive clear instructions on exactly what is expected of them. Once again, ambiguity is the enemy, and failure to enforce accountability on users' knowledge acquisition will result in poor outcomes. To that end, one of our CRM experts noted in an interview for this book that he does think there "should be an expectation to say: This is your opportunity to learn the application. We expect you to be present, paying attention and your performance after we go live is going to be indicative of how seriously you took training."[4]

This suggests some sort of evaluation should be done during launch to measure proficiency and gain an understanding of the efficacy of training or how well users were engaged. In all the mayhem of a CRM rollout, this may be impractical but could provide valuable insights. By issuing the mandate that training is expected to be treated as a priority and not an opportunity to catch up on emails, firms will realize benefits even if they cannot measure them granularly. The clear setting of the expectation of absorbing knowledge during training will help to ensure positive outcomes.

Timeliness

Research has shown that *when* training is conducted and information is disseminated may be as important as the content of the training itself. This notion, which we can call the *timeliness of training*, is defined as "the degree to which the salesperson feels that he or she received change-related training at an opportune time relative to the push for change...."[3] Admittedly, the study does not reveal exactly what that timing would be in real terms. A leading CRM consultant agreed that timeliness of training was a very important consideration and provided an additional practical insight, noting that

> Timing's pretty critical. If it's too close to launch, [users will] be fresh on the new CRM functionality but they might be disconnected from their business processes. We don't want to have them play catch-up on the launch date. You've got to get it in that sweet spot, where they have it fresh in their minds but haven't been disconnected from the business process so they have to play catch-up when the system goes live.[4]

This example highlights important insights into training in the context of a CRM launch, but we have also come to understand that firms can benefit from viewing training not as a single event related to launch, but as an ongoing facet of the overall CRM landscape. Firms may engage heavily in training initiatives during rollout and ensure that all new hires receive at least a crash course on the system, but neglect to invest in continuing education, be that in the form of refreshers of core functionality or the promotion of extended functionality which might lead to increased postadoptive use. In an environment of limited resources, we would recommend—keeping with themes explored elsewhere—that the most attention be given to reinforcing fundamentals and usage of best practices. Tim Kippley of Rightpoint Consulting underscored importance of ongoing education during our 2016 interview, reminding us that we should view CRM systems as a product and comparing ongoing training to a product adoption cycle. In his words,

> We want to keep hitting them with "hey, have you tried this? Did you see this feature where you right click here and it looks at everybody's calendar and magically finds out when everyone's available with one

click? What a cool new feature." We'll call that the ongoing feed that keeps people interested. "I learned it but I'm sure I don't remember how to do it." CRM tip of the week is another part of that. That ongoing piece which allows people to continue to learn about the system.[2]

This approach provides benefits both in the context of ensuring users continue to be proficient at using the system but also by reinforcing the value of the system and demonstrating management and the Technology Division's collective commitment to ongoing, sustained CRM success. It becomes more complicated, however, when we discover additional results from the literature, which indicate that "salespeople who think they are likely to be favorably affected by the change show a stronger preference for timely training but a weaker preference for highly structured training."[3] In other words, why are you hauling me into a conference room for three hours when I'm going to learn this on my own anyway? While it feels counterproductive to punish technologically sound self-starters, CRM adoption is a one person, one vote type of initiative. As a result, we do find ourselves with the mandate to teach to the middle, at least in the earliest stages of the user education process.

Audience

Not all trainees are created equally. Certain employees will be more technically savvy than others, and others may have a greater general *learning orientation*, defined as "the degree to which the goals of the salesperson orient him or her to improve his or her abilities and mastery of task performance."[3] Some research has shown the impact of age on the training process. Murphy et al. in 2008 and Sarin, Sego, Kohli, and Challagalla in 2010 found that older people may face anxiety about learning CRM and feel the need to ask more questions than their younger peers. At the same time, the fact that older salespeople may perceive their need for additional clarifications is interpreted by others as incompetence. A good trainer who emphasizes the appropriateness of all questions would be useful to mitigate this phenomenon and ensure salespeople of all ages walk away feeling good about their mastery of the system.

At the same time, training approaches that work best with younger salespeople can be in diametric opposition to those preferred by older salespeople, so teaching to the middle can only go so far. Without engaging in ageist activities frowned upon by Human Resources, an informal scanning of your user base to get a general sense of how experienced they are can be helpful in tailoring training decisions. For example, more mature salespeople—being less comfortable in formal environments where they are exposed to scrutiny of their potential lack of technical acumen—could gain greater understanding of CRM by being paired with a salesperson who is more comfortable with the CRM system, essentially creating a mentor–mentee relationship. The mentor does not necessarily have to be younger, but firms should be realistic in assessing who demonstrates greater competency. Ideally, super users could be paired with one or more users who are apt to prefer the mentor approach to the classroom setting. This would naturally depend on the size of the user base and the number of super users cultivated from involvement in the implementation process.

Another benefit of the mentor model is its implicit flexibility. While management should set some level of expectations to ensure that knowledge transfer is actually occurring, and implement some sort of measurement to verify, the mentor model allows users to train around their own schedules. Users who lack enthusiasm about the CRM change, or who have lower *perceived ability*—the degree of confidence salespeople have to assimilate the change—may be more apt to procrastinate. As with many areas of CRM, answering the question "What's in it for me?" will be paramount in preventing this procrastination. To ensure accountability, we may also consider some form of attestation and verification that knowledge transfer has occurred.

Curriculum

When it comes to CRM training, the Pareto principle (80/20 rule) can serve as a useful guide to developing our curriculum. The Pareto principle has multiple manifestations, but for our purposes, it states that users receive 80% of the benefits by mastering 20% of the functionality. The CRM team must look critically at all functionality and work together to arrive at the 20% which, they believe, will yield the largest benefit. This could include searching, contact entry, activity entry, list building (reports may be better handled by a support team and deployed upon request), system data levels, navigation, and pipeline management.

The urge to arm users with knowledge of every bell and whistle in the system is real, especially the urge to train on functionality that was especially challenging for the implementation team. Our goal, with initial training, however, is to plant the seeds of CRM and establish a strong foundation that will empower users with confidence in fundamentals. This foundation can provide a springboard toward self-learning and users' propensity to embrace additional system features on their own, provided that educational materials are available for doing so, such as video modules.

Types of Training

Most of the academic literature and professional insights we have discussed above center upon classroom training—led either by CRM experts or by. We also explored the benefits of the mentor model. Additional training methods exist, however, and it is useful to explore all of them to create a holistic training package that can accommodate a variety of learning styles and personalities. Tim Kippley underscored the importance of providing multiple training options, reminding us that

> people learn differently, so you want to hit the various modes in which people learn. Some people learn better in person. They aren't going to read printed material. Recorded, on-demand sessions can be useful. Others are going to be more apt to embrace coursework. These are your deeper dive folks, including Admins. These would be dedicated sessions. These sessions will be more oriented towards how the system works and why and how to administer and monitor things. It's a smaller population but it's important not to overlook those groups. We're very flexible in terms of the spectrum, but we always recommend [clients] hit the different modes in which people learn.[2]

These observations remind us that training is not only for end users of the system but also includes knowledge transfer that may need to occur between external implementation partners and internal IT resources. It is not only important to account for the broad relevant audience but also to provide multiple avenues to acquire the necessary knowledge. We will now discuss the various training vehicles in greater depth.

Classroom Training

Given the prevalence in the literature and commonness of practice, classroom training is almost certainly going to be one component of any CRM education initiative. One way trainers can expect to see greater rewards from their efforts is to avoid teaching pieces of functionality in a vacuum, but rather within the flow and structure of actual business scenarios. This applies most directly to the classroom setting, so we include it here. Scenario-based learning was a key recommendation from one CRM expert interviewed for this book. He noted the importance of doing business processes in the exact context in which they would in real life.

For example: you receive a phone call from a client, and you are going to do these seven things rather than addressing functionality piecemeal. Users need to understand the whole picture of how the system will work after it is launched. Experts also advise us to implement classroom sessions where users are sitting at their computers, working through examples real time rather than simply listening to a lecture.

Logistics Training sessions should have breaks. The environment should be comfortable. Coffee, food, and candy should be available. This is not the time to scrimp on amenities. Training is a grueling experience for both trainers and trainees (mostly for trainers). As we noted in our discussion of salesperson resistance in Chapter 2, we are dealing with the most difficult collection of corporate employees to satisfy. As groups leave training, they will inevitably gossip about the training experience to their colleagues. By making the environment comfortable, firms can do wonders to change overall user perceptions about the training experience.

A number of factors can cause firms to find themselves in time-constrained situations when the training portion of the life cycle rolls around. Perhaps go-live timelines have been moved. Perhaps conference room reservation constraints suggest that we should blast through all the sessions as quickly as possible. We cannot underestimate the impact, however, of running trainers into the ground. Even small breaks to let trainers leave the room can have significant benefits and improve their stamina and quality of training.

Training Guides and Cheat Sheets

The training guide is a paradox of CRM implementations. It feels like a mandatory exercise, but also like throwaway work. After all, most of us would prefer to get live, real-time help via a face-to-face conversation than sift through a book full of bullet points and screenshots. If your organization is able to employ technical writers or can devote other resources to the training guide, it certainly does not hurt to create, but an extensive tome is by no means mandatory. The structure and culture of your organization will play a large role in whether you will need to create a training manual. Larger, more structured organizations tend to prefer to spend effort on training manual creation, whereas smaller companies often opt for a collection of smaller, tactical means to educate users such as those outlined below.

One counterintuitive approach to training guide creation is to document some of the more advanced functionality available to users within the system. Since we are going to devote most of our formal training to the most important 20% of functionality, a training guide is a good means to capture some portion of the other 80%. Users who fail to completely absorb everything provided in formal training are most likely to eventually acquire that information organically through conversations with their colleagues or perhaps through interactions with the support team.

Even though the functionality outlined in the training guide may be intimidating, the brevity of the guide makes it feel more accessible. Laminated cheat sheets may be beneficial. Key terms and core concepts are good candidates for laminated cheat sheets. These should be reviewed during a live setting rather than simply disseminated at random. For documentation to be absorbed most effectively, it should be previewed verbally, distributed one piece at a time, and discussed succinctly. This discussion has focused primarily on non-digital collateral. The tangibility of handing users information has shown itself to be beneficial in knowledge acquisition. As we continue to enhance our CRM system over time, we can always inform users of changes and provide brief training notes via email and internal intranets.

Video Modules

Certain audiences will benefit more from and naturally prefer targeted chunks of information. We know from our research that more mature salespeople, in particular, have been shown to be more resistant to live training as they may fear being seen as lacking technical prowess and may even fear for their jobs if others believe they lag behind their colleagues in this increasingly important area of technical literacy. Similar to more mature salespeople, Tim Kippley notes that senior members of an organization may say that they are too busy or even important to attend training sessions, though these hesitations may actually also be the result of fear of being seen as inept. Senior people in the firm might not want to expose themselves to that especially if they have not been close to the project or are not technically savvy. But in the privacy of their offices, they will watch a 2 min tutorial that is contextually relevant.

These tutorials are composed of voice narration coupled with recordings of screen actions and can be posted on a firm's intranet and also referenced during classroom trainings, on team calls, and via email postings. Modules will be best embraced in an organization that places a premium on self-sufficiency. As new users join the firm, referring them to training modules will be less taxing on support resources and on the new users' colleagues, who can ask that their new peers review the video modules prior to engaging with questions.

Efficiency and Best Practices

Even firms that consider training to be a high priority and focus on creating many ways to facilitate their users' ability to learn may omit what one leading CRM consultant considered to be some of the most important information any CRM user could acquire: tips on efficiency and usage of best practices. Despite their criticality, these tips are easy to omit especially because trainers and project team members are likely using most of them subconsciously and they would not be naturally top of mind and feel like they should be added to a formal curriculum. During a 2016 interview, the

CRM consultant referenced above explained the situation he often observes, noting,

> What's missing from a lot of training is best practices—tips and tricks on how to work in the system. We spend so much time being official and formal and getting all our documentation just right to hand over to the users that we forget to say 'hey, by the way, you can right-click, you can hover' and these are the things that are going to make a big difference in how someone uses the CRM.[4]

For example, some hosted CRM solutions perform best in Google Chrome, and others in Firefox or Internet Explorer. Ensuring that users have knowledge of the best browser to use to yield the greatest performance and presentation benefits is an example of how a small piece of knowledge can yield exponential benefits over time manifested as reduced frustration and greater efficiency. Is it easier to operate the CRM using multiple browser windows or multiple tabs? Are there hot keys that can help users navigate the system more effectively or reduce click counts? Users benefit with every interaction with the CRM system by knowing a few simple items.

One of the biggest hurdles to the adoption challenge is a system where users are not easily able to achieve flow, are sidetracked by extraneous clicks or hovers that appear when we do not want them to, or forgetting to, work with multiple instances of the CRM open, as noted by our consultant above. Users may know how to enter a phone call, but they do not know the *best* way to enter the call, in the context of how the system operates more broadly. The cumulative effect of the inefficiency will cause harm to ongoing adoption and attempts to create system advocates.

Chapter Summary

In this chapter, we have explored the vast landscape of considerations firms should evaluate when planning user education initiatives. We have learned that timing, voluntariness, and management cues about training are important precursors to training success. We have examined key mental paradigms which can be implemented to improve users' likelihood to absorb material and walk away from training with increased confidence about the system. One of these principles, the expectation effect, yields results when trainers and peers use words like "easy" or "simple" when discussing the CRM system. As a corollary, users' perceived ability and thus perceived ease of use of the system increase. Returning to TAM, we recall that the variable PEOU influences user perceptions of usefulness (PU), which subsequently influences users' attitudes and behavioral intentions to use the system.

We have examined CRM educational curriculum in the context of the Pareto principle (80/20 rule), and we posit that understanding 20% of the CRM system's functionality will yield 80% of the benefits for users. We also now understand that different modes of training have shown themselves to be effective including classroom training, video modules, and printed cheat sheets. Firms can benefit from striking a balance between devoting resources to creating large volumes of formal documentation versus more tactical collateral which may be more consumable to an audience with many conflicting demands surrounding their jobs and how CRM plays into them.

We further understand that understanding certain factors about our user audience such as maturity and level of experience can help shape decisions surrounding which modes of training should be promoted to which users.

References

1. Clark, P., Rocco, R. A., & Bush, A. J. (2007). Sales force automation systems and sales force productivity: Critical issues and research agenda. *Journal of Relationship Marketing 6(2)*, 67–87.
2. Kippley, T. & Schneider, B. (2016, February 18). CRM practitioners—Rightpoint. (S. J. Kinnett, Interviewer).
3. Sarin, S., Sego, T., Kohli, A. K., & Challagalla, G. (2010). Characteristics that enhance training effectiveness in implementing technological change in sales strategy: A field-based exploratory study. *Journal of Personal Selling & Sales Management 30(2)*, 143–156.
4. Anonymous. (2016, January 12–13). Making CRM successful—CRM practitioner interview. (S. J. Kinnett, Interviewer).

15

BIG DATA, STEWARDSHIP, AND ANALYTICS

With the growing popularity of big data, analytics, and the lure of the promise of the ability to predict customer behavior, organizations are exploring the utilization of external data providers and data stewards in addition to constructing data warehouses to combine data across multiple systems including customer relationship management (CRM). In this chapter, we will explore key concepts in big data and analytics and how these concepts can manifest themselves within the context of CRM implementation. We will next examine data stewardship both in the context of internal and external stewardship. Finally, we will examine the emerging landscape of external, supplemental data providers.

The Big Data Revolution

Take a look at marketing collateral for any major CRM vendor and you will see references to analytics capabilities. Anecdotally, water cooler conversations also seem to point to big data as the hot topic for organizations looking for competitive advantage. It is the new shiny toy and it has caught the attention of many executives. Research suggests, however, that a disconnect likely exists between chief information officers (CIOs) and other executives and managers. To that end, a 2014 examination of big data perceptions found that "thirty seven percent of [CIOs] surveyed said that big data was a 'low or below-average' priority."[1] CIOs have a unique position in that they have greater exposure to implementation details and possess an understanding of the cost and resourcing requirements necessary for big data initiatives compared to other C-level executives. This vantage point has colored their perceptions—as noted in the 2014 study—that the general landscape of big data is immature, overhyped, and viewed more as a technology initiative than a holistic business initiative. CIOs might be onto something.

The promise of endless commercial insights and buying pattern predictions is so alluring that CRM is at risk of being perverted into a one stop shop for all possible data points. As we know from our exploration of system design and best practices, less is more, and the promise of big data threatens to derail that core philosophy. This sentiment is not without support from the professional CRM community. Both consultants interviewed for this book cautioned that the lust for big data comes with risks of compromising user experience and subsequently adoption. Tim Kippley of Chicago-headquartered Rightpoint Consulting noted:

> The risk [of sacrificing CRM product quality] is real because big data really is a hot topic right now. It's not just big data but the recommendation engines coming on the market. And there is absolutely value there. But most importantly—CRM is about understanding what users need to do and making it easier for users to accomplish those tasks. So ultimately, you never want to do something that compromises the user experience for the sake of data.[2]

The notion that big data initiatives are technology driven is a key insight to our discussion. When viewed through this lens, some organizations may find themselves lobbying the Technology Division to beef up its data capture abilities "just in case" they are needed for emerging analytics initiatives. Devoting some resources to exploring the creation of a data warehouse to capture existing fields, or a subset of existing fields, may be worth exploring for firms with manageable data sets. The CIO perceptions noted above inform our approach by highlighting the importance of a big data road map and corresponding strategy preceding technology decisions.

In order to ensure the results of big data initiatives justify the burden on users, firms must be able to show that the analytics directly serve those entering the data. They need to understand the goal is not simply management reporting. They must understand that their contributions will yield significant commercial results and users should in many cases be incentivized to enter the data points deemed necessary to succeed in a big data initiative. One reason we must be especially guarded in our pursuit of these big data initiatives is they have the potential to compromise adoption. As we increase the number of checkboxes and required fields on the theory that we might eventually find a use for them within a data warehouse, adoption of the system will almost certainly decrease. A number of the design principles we have explored underscore this risk. Hick's law has shown us that the more functionality that exists, the longer it will take to complete a given task. Users must also make decisions about the actual values they will enter in these extra fields. As a result, fewer data points will be entered into the system, resulting in less effective data analytics. Moreover, all of the other benefits organizations would reap as the result of successful adoption are also at risk. It is not too dramatic to suggest that an overzealous big data initiative could have sweeping consequences on achieving CRM success.

To prevent this, firms should develop clear, concise goals for their analytics strategy. Algorithms should be defined and an inventory of data points necessary to achieve these goals should be created. This information should be presented to the CRM governance team for discussion. In this forum, the translation between the analytics goals and the CRM implementation details may be understood and if the changes are deemed not to be too burdensome for users, they can be prioritized for development. What is clear is that a "shoot first, ask questions later" analytics approach will almost certainly compromise your CRM. Once incorrect, burdensome implementation decisions have been deployed, regaining adoption can be challenging if not impossible. Once a user has concluded the system is too difficult, in the absence of draconian system usage mandates, it will be difficult to regain the user's commitment while simultaneously generating disgust and cynicism, which will permeate the rest of the sales force.

Firms that have already waded into the big data swamp by beefing up their CRM data capture mechanisms could benefit from taking pause. One mechanism which could be used to understand whether you have implemented a system which is clogged with extraneous fields is to perform simple data analysis to understand what percentage of each given field is populated. If you find—to take an extreme example—a contact's FAX number has been filled in <1% of the time, it should likely be removed and such information relegated to a catch-all "What's Important" type of free text field. Some conventional wisdom cautions against the use of catch-all fields, but FAX number—outside of the analysis of its necessity—does not hold value in reporting or analytics initiatives. Prior to its potential decommission, it could be useful to schedule the usage report to be run on a periodic basis and discussed by the CRM Governance Committee. Firms often focus on new features or extended functionality but the removal of outdated, underutilized, or ancillary functionality might well be a better use of time and resources.

Is it useful to notify users before removing fields? Maybe. While the loss of control of having a system change without consent could be frustrating, for fields that are grossly underused, a dialogue might invite one user who does populate the field to argue for its retention even though it is useless to others and is clutter on the UI and adds no value to analytics. Because of the functionality–usability trade-off, we know that every means we can use to simplify the user-interface results in better chances of increased adoption, which in turn will improve the results of the CRM initiative. Once the clutter has been culled and a lean and clean interface has been restored, firms may then begin—from a business and not technology posture—to examine the specific big data goals they have. After developing a concise mission, they can reengage with Technology and begin to craft an implementation approach.

Data Stewardship and External Data Sources

As the volume of CRM data increases, firms have begun to examine various methods of data stewardship be it internally or with the aid of external data stewards. Recall from our discussion of CRM governance, data stewardship is the area in which some firms have embraced governance models even if they have yet to implement these models to manage broader strategic and system architecture decisions. Some aspects of data stewardship are implicit in basic CRM usage. Entering phone calls and meetings qualify as data stewardship. Updating outdated phone numbers is another example as is merging duplicate contacts. Ensuring opportunity/pipeline records reflect current realities about estimated close date, expected revenue, and changes in products being pitched are all useful data stewardship exercises. To the latter, we can see *only* an employee—not an external provider—would have knowledge to maintain those data points. As a result, we understand that external data stewards will be necessarily limited in the data points they can manage, which is one factor that will drive our decision-making surrounding the potential procurement of such stewards.

First, Look Inward

In a thriving, well-adopted CRM system, the need for external data stewards would typically be quite low. Users who see value in their CRM will be naturally inclined to keep it clean and well-functioning, allowing them to work more efficiently. Much of the data that users will be maintaining will be data they themselves have put into the system, but users may be less-inclined to dig through other data sources to enrich their existing data. The promise of supplementary information—as much as the stewardship of core CRM information—is part of the growing appeal of external data stewards.

As we have seen, realizing a thriving, well-adopted CRM system is no small task, but we would encourage firms to look to gamification and incentives to rally internal employees to become better stewards before looking for external sources. Gamification initiatives will almost certainly be cheaper and also bring the key benefit of allowing users to retain control—something we know is critical to hedging against user resistance. At the same time, we can recall from an earlier chapter that we cited research suggesting one challenge with achieving CRM adoption was the reality that salespeople are often asked to do too much administrative work. As a result, users may interpret engaging with CRM as a chore rather something that adds value to the sales process, leading to role conflict and all its related negative outcomes.

Given this real and significant risk of administrative work leading to poor adoption, it may seem as if external data stewardship is an obvious choice, especially when we hear of so many purported benefits. We will see below a key observation about the high variance of competency among external data stewards, but in the event that we can secure a competent external data steward, it may well help inform us of emerging developments in the marketplace. Despite all of our best efforts, we may not have the internal resources to devote to analyzing emerging options coming into the market. An expert CRM practitioner suggests the benefits to external data stewards should be viewed as part of a longer-term strategy, noting that "ten, fifteen years ago we didn't know about Twitter, gathering customer data, giving that sort of voice to customers. We have no clue what's coming on the market in the next ten years. Using the right data provider can put you in a better position to be ahead of these trends."[3]

Control

We have explored the importance of control and the frustration that results when users feel they are not in control. Enlisting the aid of external data stewards clearly represents a loss of control for the user base. On the one hand, administrative work might go down, but what if stewards make mistakes or make changes without sufficient notifications, or if notifications become so frequent that the overhead of reading them begins to exceed the effort that salespeople would have expended to manage the data themselves? All of these considerations should give organizations pause as they begin to evaluate external data stewardship. These considerations also point to the need for clearly delineated responsibilities for external stewards and internal users and the necessity of assertive service-level agreements and an assumption of excellence on the part of external stewards. A CRM expert highlighted, during a 2016 interview, the difference between potential and reality for some data providers:

> Conceptually [external data stewards] are a great idea. Having someone else who can provide you complementary, supplementary information about their customers is valuable. However, a lot of these intermediary data providers aren't very good at what they do, unfortunately. So it's a balance. You have to find the right data partners. A lot of them talk a big talk on the pre-sales side but once you get into an implementation you realize they have no clue what they're doing.[3]

This sentiment underscores the immaturity of the external data steward market. Given the technical overhead of bringing in external stewards and building all the necessary data integrations, choosing an incompetent steward opens a firm to drastic consequences. Depending on the severity of the missteps, regaining user adoption could be near impossible. Consider all the complexities of intraorganizational system integration—noted in an earlier chapter as one of the riskiest and most difficult aspects of most CRM implementations—and expand those complexities to integration initiatives with external providers and we are left with arguably the highest risk portion of a CRM project. Limiting the scope of the quantity of data and the tasks performed on data by external stewards could have some effect on mitigating risk.

When engaging external data stewards, it is important to be very specific in the functions your organization seeks to outsource. Firms will benefit from drawing clear lines between internal and external data stewardship expectations and responsibilities. Tim Kippley of Chicago-based Rightpoint Consulting recommends using external vendors to streamline purely administrative functions but drawing the line at function needing organizational knowledge to be addressed properly. Depending on the industry, we might be talking about a small subset of total information that can be trusted to those without specific business knowledge. In such cases, weighing the costs of insourcing these data tasks is worthwhile. Kippley extended this point, noting that

> People need proper knowledge of the business to be true data owners. People within the organization can say "I know I met with this person and that interaction isn't in the system." Someone who's not part of the organization won't have that context so they'll only be able to make the best decision they can. [External data stewards or data providers] can provide a cost-effective way of managing certain information but the critical decisions still need to be made within the organization.[2]

While we understand users are not necessarily clamoring to own every single data point in the system, the manipulation of certain pieces of data such as phone number or address have the potential to cause significant frustration if external data stewards make mistakes. Back to our earlier sentiment about the high variability in competence of external data stewards, firms could benefit by asking stewards to maintain a small number of fields and assess their competence over time before expanding their remit.

Given our understanding that no external steward will have the expertise of an internal user when it comes to certain data points, a natural part of any external stewardship implementation is the delineation of responsibilities. We must inventory the objects and fields we want to be handled by the external stewards and we must come to agreement on how often the fields will be updated, from what data repository the fields are being sourced, and how changes to these fields will be communicated to internal users, if at all. Another consideration will be whether fields will become totally locked for internal users or if they have the option to overwrite external stewards' decisions. If auditing features are available within your CRM, the fields which can be touched by external data stewards would be excellent candidates for auditing. As always, we want to minimize the number of fields we audit, lest the list become too unmanageable, but this would be an example of a worthy auditing decision.

Communication and Timing

What criteria will determine *when* fields will be populated? Event driven? Periodically based on an agreed-upon window of time? What notification, if any, will inform users to changes in their data, and what will be the frequency of those notifications? The benefit of notifications, in general, is largely predicated on the frequency decision. We would suggest that the quantity of notifications be proportional to the criticality of timeliness of the data change. For example, if a user needs to take immediate action on the data update, an event-driven communication could be useful.

If data updates pertain to basic reference data—phone numbers, addresses, and so on—a weekly summary communication of the past week's data update could be the appropriate volume of communications. It is also important that service-level agreements are clear to end users for situations where they submit requests for data updates. This typically occurs when a field has been locked and designated as an item that is completely managed by the external data provider.

Chapter Summary

As this chapter draws to a close, some may feel that we have thrown a wet blanket on what is arguably one of the most exciting promises of CRM as of this book's publication. We have heard so much about the importance of robust analytics programs and harnessing the power of big data to reap large commercial gains. We do not dispute that—when executed correctly—big data may yield positive organizational outcomes. As we have seen, however, both from research and expert opinions, organizations that have not mastered operational CRM fundamentals are poorly positioned to succeed with their big data initiatives. Attempting to dive into big data without achieving said operational mastery risks frustrating users, managers, and technologists alike. We want organizations to succeed with big data but not at the expense of adoption and effective sales force automation.

We also explored considerations surrounding external data stewards. We can see that external data providers or data stewards have value but—given what we have seen about the efficacy of many such vendors and the constraints on what we can comfortably outsource to them—it would be difficult to conclude they are mandatory or even always helpful. We agree data must be kept clean, but who does it remains a very valid question. Considering these providers can be part of your CRM assessment but designing a system that addresses core user needs such as usability remains a higher priority. We would posit that, as of the writing of this book, external stewardship remains in its infancy and should be considered as a high-risk, moderate-reward initiative. As the industry matures, we can hope to see benefits increase.

References

1. Barwick, H. (2014, April 30). CIOs still want to keep IT in-house. Retrieved August 14, 2014, from CIO. http://www.cio.com.au/article/print/544001/cios_still_want_to_keep_it_in-house/.
2. Kippley, T., & Schneider, B. (2016, February 18). CRM practitioners—Rightpoint (S. J. Kinnett, Interviewer).
3. Anonymous. (2016, January 12–13). Making CRM successful—CRM practitioner interview (S. J. Kinnett, Interviewer).

16
SUPPORT

Throughout our discussions of salesperson resistance and cynicism, lack of application support has been cited as a critical mistake in resourcing decisions and a key contributor to user frustration and ultimately customer relationship management (CRM) failure. Support positions have at times been viewed diminutively as lower-level positions with undefined growth paths except perhaps to manage other support personnel. This phenomenon is surprising given what research has shown us about the criticality of delivering timely, friendly, and accurate support. Investing in a support team is an especially important component of achieving CRM success. In fact, in the event that your firm is unable or unwilling to make a large technology product investment, consider making the business case for increasing your support team both in headcount and efficiency. Whether the latter involves time off task by building more scalable support tools, leading training sessions, or implementing a superuser model is at your discretion.

In the last few years, some firms have begun to understand exactly how important the support role has become given its causal connection to adoption, as discussed already. Studies conducted by the noted HR consulting firm Mercer and IT research firm Gartner and referenced in a 2013 article in *ComputerWorld* noted that in 2014, the help desk was listed as one of the top four "hot jobs" on the horizon for the new year. The help desk has become more sophisticated than in the past, having undergone a shift in orientation—as noted by Stacy Collett in her exploration of the help desk for *ComputerWorld*—"from order taker to problem-solver"[1]. This trend is as prevalent in government as it is in the business sector. David Stevens, CIO of Maricopa County, Arizona, underscored this point in a 2013 interview with *ComputerWorld*, noting that his team no longer just takes calls and triages tickets but also is now empowered to dig in and solve problems as they are presented.

Writing in the same article for *ComputerWorld*, Collett noted that the help desk has the potential to be a real competitive advantage for many organizations. In an organization that structures the support function to be collaborative with the business analysis function and encourages feedback loops, insights gleaned from the support function can be fed directly back to both managers and business analysts and potentially drive decisions for future enhancements. To that end, it is critical that support personnel be empowered to capture, reflect upon, and ultimately pass insights along to others. Support personnel often have the best handle on exactly what pains users are facing and—if given proper voice within the organization—could contribute insights to evaluating the most appropriate projects going forward. Devaluating the voice of the support team, and thus the user base, could result in a CRM initiative driven too heavily by management, who are often far too disconnected to be effective in addressing some of the user pain points that, when remedied, put firms on a path back to adoption.

Transitioning from Implementation to Support

As noted during our discussion of postadoptive and extended use, we cannot rely very long on the implementation teams to provide support. One interviewee noted that application support is not always a strength of an implementation team. While it would be unreasonable for consultants to run immediately after going live, neither should we expect to lean on them for too long. As a result, organizations must plan ahead and have a clearly defined support model and sufficient human capital to execute on the model efficiently and effectively.

The ideal CRM support team member must rate highly in both interpersonal and technical skills. One reason help desks (not exactly analogous to an application support team, despite being interchanged colloquially) have been such breeding grounds for resentment and frustration is they have in some cases failed to make staffing decisions which adequately take into account these dual requirements. Ultimately, however, no matter how skilled, charismatic, or popular a support representative is, he will probably not ever gain the level of credibility that a salesperson who has achieved system mastery will when it comes to helping his colleagues. We discussed how users involved in the implementation process become natural superusers. The ideal superuser model does not allow superusers to disappear after an implementation is completed but rather integrates them as valuable members of an ongoing commitment to success via the support function. We will now examine exactly how important superusers are as system support resources.

Superusers as Support

We recommend implementing a superuser model whenever possible as a component of a support team. The superuser model is effective in that it leverages existing human capital and—implemented correctly—does not negatively impact the user from performing his original business function. The ideal superuser has above-average technical acumen and is not overstretched on other initiatives. These individuals should be selected on their natural skills rather than by forced compliance. Some folks are more predisposed to enjoy tasks like training and learning about technology. If you—or a trusted colleague—have a good pulse of your sales organization, you should be able to identify those individuals.

Issue Tracking

Issue tracking is a necessary but sometimes frustrating facet of CRM support both for users and the support team. This is largely a result of the way tickets are constructed. Support teams operate most efficiently when they have clearly defined support requests submitted in a uniform fashion through a tracking system, which allows them to prioritize, triage, and resolve requests quickly and accurately. Getting users to utilize support tickets instead of desk visits, phone calls, or instant messages is a key component of the broader system adoption challenge. Failing to achieve process discipline when it comes to support will alienate both users and support personnel alike.

Achieving CRM success in the support space (a precondition to broader CRM success) is predicated on the cultivation of an environment where users are able to submit information quickly, support personnel will be able to address issues accurately, and users will walk away feeling empowered to reengage with the system. In a prior chapter, we discussed Hick's law and its application to the design of screens within the CRM system. Support tickets are an area ripe for over-architecture with screens sometimes triggering negative emotions even upon a quick glance. The fundamental problem is analogous to the problem with those overly concerned with big data: believing information needs to be tracked when it really does not. The same principles we have discussed apply again. Can we answer the question: "What specific decision and action will be taken as a result of this aggregated data?" We will now explore how it is not just the composition of the tickets themselves but also the context in which tickets are submitted to collectively determine our approach.

To begin with, if a user needs to submit a support ticket, his or her emotional state is already one of frustration. After all, the system is not working properly. The user is unable to do what is necessary to perform his or her vital business functions. The user wishes he could send an instant message, make a phone call, slap some text into an email, and receive personal attention from a support representative or project team member, but in many cases is required, or at least encouraged, to complete a ticket instead. When a user is presented with a support ticket packed with fields, the resulting cynicism will make him regret following the appropriate support process and, where possible, walk over to a support representative's desk, send an instant message, or otherwise break the preferred process. Since tickets need to be entered anyway, the onus then falls on the support representative, who is unlikely to send a user back to his or her desk unaided. The result is a support team flustered by the need to enter tickets on a user's behalf.

In some cases, users may even be unable to complete required fields present on support tickets and, as a result, fill them with garbage or, as noted above, abandon the process altogether. From a user's perspective, he or she needs little more than a textbox to type the issue details. From a support perspective, we would like to have a few other fields—Assignee, Status (in progress, waiting for others, and so on). To that end, there is nothing wrong with implementing support ticketing as the primary mechanism for users to solicit support. It is absolutely necessary to get a picture of the universe of support requests, which is predicated by designing and managing tickets effectively. The design should ensure rapid issue resolution as well as knowledge capture to understand which issues occur the most often and ideally how to get out in front of these issues going forward.

Applying Hick's Law to Support Tickets

Users are already diverting their attention from their intended CRM tasks to request support. The larger the cognitive load placed on them to complete each ticket, the less likely they will be to devote their full attention to effectively capturing the issue. Screenshots, error messages, and well-crafted descriptions of issues—all of these have the potential to suffer if users are distracted by populating extraneous information, which is less likely to provide rapid issue resolution. Recall that Hick's law states that "the time required to make a decision is a function of the number of available options."[2] Most firms will find that, upon reflection and analysis, the list of fields required to effectively address a support request is actually quite small. We will now explore a few classic fields typically found in support tickets, which we would argue are unnecessary and subsequently provide an example of a simple but effective field inventory.

Title

A thoroughly bizarre field choice which is sometimes mandatory in some packaged systems with support ticket functionality is "Title" or "Name." The essence of the support request can be captured in the first line of the body of text where users populate details of their requests. In the heat of the support ticket submission process, what sort of insights do we expect to gain from user-defined issue titles? Ticket titles, like email subject lines, range from "HELP" to "BROKEN" to "Please address ASAP" and do little to provide value. We recommend omitting this field.

Location

Another field sometimes found in a support ticket is "Location" or something of that nature. Perhaps for larger firms with geographic dispersion, the intent is to triage issues more effectively and allow for desk visits. This information, however, could be maintained on a user record and calculated upon submission or cross-referenced (depending on the system's capabilities) later, eliminating the need for it to be populated on the screen.

Priority

Priority is another field sometimes found on support tickets. But let us not pretend that user-specified priority rankings influence the way we triage and address support requests. How many users deem their requests to be low priority? Not many. User-driven assessment of priority is comical. What user's priority is not bright red critical? One alternative to the conventional wisdom about ticket prioritization would be to allow the support team to assign priority at its discretion. These assignments would be shielded from users. Another option would be to mandate priority only if a specific escalation or cross-team collaboration will be needed. Examples of this scenario include the need to loop-in database administrators, infrastructure analysts, or outside vendors. The very inclusion of a priority sets these items apart. Consider removing the priority field altogether. As we know from prior analysis, the cumulative effect of chipping away at the total number of fields per screen will ensure better results.

Time to Completion

Do not ever require time to completion. It seems to be one of the most popular yet most damaging field on support tickets. One difficulty inherent in this choice is the reality that often several individuals participate in the process of resolving a particular support ticket. Especially in the immediate aftermath of a deployment when project team members are still quite embedded in the support function, by the time the task is completed, each member would need to opine on the time it took to complete. A support request might require input from a business analyst to provide insight on the initial requirement or business context. A user might weigh in to clarify his or her original question. One or more engineers might be required to remedy the task along with a system administrator. With a straight face, can we really say that the cumulative time is easy to capture or even possible at all?

The result is pure guesswork that achieves nothing, and suddenly we have created a field that both adds overhead to the support process and is also useless. We must ask ourselves: is sitting around thinking about how long we spent working on something really the best use of time?

We would posit that it is sufficient to measure quantity of requests to gain insights about the level of support required, but if organizations truly insist on segmenting tickets based on effort, we would suggest a field such as "level of complexity"—high, medium, and low. A formula assigning a static number of minutes per ranking could then be applied and would likely be far closer to reality than support resources' best guesses. Perhaps even a binary distinction—easy or hard—could be useful. These types of decisions significantly impact how efficiently support tickets can be managed. We would posit that many practitioners would agree that the very thought of working a support queue causes a negative visceral response. This is largely a result of how overwhelming the tickets are to review and manage.

Categorization

Support requests are often multifaceted and could be linked to data integration, application errors, training issues, and other areas. Attempting to categorize these, particularly early in the process, adds little value and in some cases is not even possible as in situations where many factors are involved. Some may argue such categorization is encompassed in the realm of "best practices," but what has shown such practices truly are the best? If quantity of issues reported could lead to the prioritization of certain improvement initiatives then perhaps our recommendation might be different. The reality is that, even armed with these data, stakeholders are often drawn to more glamorous projects.

To further underscore our caution surrounding over-categorization, consider that cognitively, we want to have lists contain the same structure of information. For example, if we chose to categorize by object (e.g., Account, Contact, Opportunity, and so on), we limit ourselves. What if an issue impacts multiple objects? We could use a multiselect list, though in many cases the visual presentation of such lists is less than ideal and also creates reporting challenges. There could be benefit in segmenting these items so they could be assigned to resources supporting those integrated products. This breaks our category structure and underscores the importance of being thoughtful about exactly what we hope to get from categorization.

One particular area that makes lives miserable is subcategorization. First, we should be clear that if we succeed in limiting the number of values in the Category field, but require a subcategory, we completely undermine the benefits of simplifying the Category. In fact, we would be better off, from an efficiency perspective, using only Category and—if we must—populating it with more values rather than to require sub-values. It is as if we are being punished for taking time to categorize our tickets. We must not lose sight of our goal, which is to understand, action, and close support tickets as quickly and accurately as possible while retaining insights to help us run our business effectively. Anything that does not facilitate those goals is ancillary and hindering.

Chapter Summary

In this chapter, we have explored the nature of the support function. Once viewed diminutively, firms are increasingly realizing the value that the support team can provide and they increasingly see a robust support function as a source of competitive advantage. We then explored the nature of the ideal support resource. Those best-positioned to deliver high caliber support are those who rate high in both technical acumen and interpersonal skills. While at times off-shoring the support function was commonplace, more and more organizations have learned that potential communication barriers are more than just irritating but could result in compromised CRM adoption.

The context of support calls is already one of high stress and everything from fuzzy connections, misunderstood speech, or untimely resolutions can spike user resentment and that resentment explodes not just against the provider of support but also the CRM system itself (already a subject of some level of resentment since it precipitated the need for the support call). The cynicism and resentment further expand to CRM champions and colleagues who have evangelized the tool. Recall from our discussion of social behaviors and subjective norm that—in the presence of high resentment—system advocates and evangelists will come under fire from colleagues. The potential for such far-reaching ramifications has contributed to moves to onshore the support function, invest in human capital, and provide more attractive career paths to entice the highest caliber individuals to join up.

We next explored the technical side of support with specific attention given to issue-tracking mechanisms. We have seen that support tickets—despite being crafted by and for system administrators and their support colleagues—nevertheless often fall victim to the same mistakes in over-architecture, which plague other areas of the system. Perhaps as a result of a need to justify resourcing, some support tickets attempt to utilize foolish metrics such as "time to completion," which we have seen is almost certainly populated inaccurately given the natural inability to, in hindsight, provide estimates about tasks which may have been completed weeks in the past.

Overall, we have arrived at an understanding that despite our best efforts during implementation, the nature of CRM will require robust support, but not necessarily in the ways some may think. Unwinding the over-architecture of the support function to streamline processes, reduce the amount of effort required to solicit support and no longer pretending that all metrics are useful will take time, but these initiatives are not as complicated as they seem. Begin by reviewing exactly what decisions are being made as a result of the information we capture. If we cannot point to specific decisions, we should begin paring the fields until we arrive at a manageable universe, which truly reflects the needs of the business and makes it easier for users to get help with CRM.

References

1. Collett, S. (2013, December 16). The help desk is hot again. *ComputerWorld* 17–19.
2. Lidwell, W., Holden, K., & Butler, J. (2010). *Universal Principles of Design*. Beverly, MA: Rockport.

17

EXTENDED AND POSTADOPTIVE USE

When firms think about the typical customer relationship management (CRM) implementation life cycle, they may consider a CRM initiative complete a month or so after deployment. Once initial training initiatives have concluded, support volumes have stabilized, and users have generally gained competence, it is on to the next project. Certainly, some attention remains on CRM: new fields to be added, reports to be built, and management projects to be evaluated. But one area that, if focused upon, could yield increased return on CRM investment is the encouragement of what can be called extended or postadoptive use. A 2011 study underscored this point, noting that "once [Operational CRM] technology has been successfully implemented and utilized on a regular basis, managers should shift their attention beyond mandatory use and encourage higher-level usage behavior, such as extended use, in order to maximize the returns of the technologies in which they have invested."[1]

Theoretical frameworks to ground this discussion are sparse. The technology acceptance model (TAM) seems like a probable candidate to evaluate postadoption, but as Clark, Rocco, and Bush noted in a 2007 study, one limitation of the TAM, however, is that it "does not specifically measure the extent of technology usage, which is important to help understand technology usage and continued use behavior."[2] When we think about extended use, we are referring to whether employees have bought-in to the technology and are willing to take initiative to learn more complicated functions than just the basics needed to satisfy management requirements or perform their base job requirements.

Extended use is a choice made by—in our case—salespeople and other users of our CRM system, which manifests when users have overcome initial resistance, mastered mandatory functionality, and have moved to a cognitive place where they have become open to the system providing value to them. Answering the key question "What's in it for me?" during earlier phases of the implementation can be effective in providing the cognitive space necessary for users later to embrace extended use. Extended use can also be encouraged through incentives and gamification, as well as through expanded training curriculum. Either during the launch process or via ongoing sessions, providing visibility into the wealth of functions available to users within the system is a good first step toward enabling users to pursue extended use. A 2011 study provided an example of the impact of extended use within the customer service space, noting that extended use can "enhance service employees' capacity to satisfy customers, which in turn contributes to [employees'] performance outcomes."[1] As with our other research, we can extend insights from any particular user group to other user groups. In this example, the research focused on customer satisfaction via the customer service function. In the sales context, we may draw a direct parallel. Salespeople who embrace extended use will likely gain both operational benefits and customer benefits as they uncover insights which better allow them to tailor their approach to customers' needs. This will presumably result in increased sales, thereby advancing a salesperson's career.

Extended use may manifest, in practical terms, as users engaging in report building or other advanced CRM functions which are sometimes considered the realm of Technology or a business support function. Any use of the CRM system beyond the mandatory acts of logging interactions and maintaining client reference data could be considered extended use—even something as simple as utilizing optional fields because users have identified a way to make them relevant to their sales process. This represents a brief surrender to the intent of the software: to provide opportunities to improve sales process through effective technical implementation.

Technology Quality and User Feedback

The prevailing paradigm of superior CRM technology which we have positioned throughout this book appears specifically within post-adoption literature. As we discussed in Chapter 1, CRM advice that leans too heavily on process and strategy without acknowledging the

criticality of technology quality (which can be viewed as the aggrega-
tion of many specific decisions ranging from the infrastructure which
influences internet connection speed to database optimization to user
configuration complexity to interface design decisions and beyond) is
incomplete. In the context of achieving extended and postadoptive
CRM use, "unfavorable [technology] quality signals can destructively
introduce a vicious learning cycle such that employees are unwilling
to expand their knowledge and use of the additional functions in the
installed technology."[1]

Ideally, we would avoid falling into this cycle altogether, but if we
do find ourselves there, we do have options to escape. Extricating
ourselves from the cycle can be achieved through user engagement
and active feedback solicitation. Although user feedback may manifest as complaints about known issues, it is the very process of solicit-
ing, listening, and empathizing with the feedback which provides the
first foothold to disrupt negative perceptions of the CRM technology. In fact, better to act as if the feedback is novel and previously
unknown than to placate users with "it's a known issue" which does
nothing to add credibility to the problem. If anything, it reduces
user confidence in the technology organization for leaving problems unaddressed. We explored the importance of user involvement
throughout the implementation cycle, but we can now see that the
benefits of such involvement do not end at system rollout, but such
involvement also serves as a critical component of the postadoptive
stage, with one study noting that "if we conceive IT implementation
as an extended learning process, user participation that helps to elicit
user insights is a valuable practice throughout the various stages of
IT implementation...."[1]

As we think back to our discussion of success and how it is defined,
firms may be incorrectly concluding that the CRM has not yielded a
financial return on investment, even though employees are only using
core functionality. It is true, however, that core functionality must be
robust and 80% of usage will be usage of core functionality. It is that
remaining 20% of functionality which may bring firms the ultimate
competitive advantage in the market. Let us not misinterpret this as a
recommendation to add more bells and whistles to CRM, but rather
to understand that as users become comfortable with well-designed
and implemented core functionality—such as the basic sales force

automation features including contact management, activity tracking, call list generation, and customer segmentation—they will be more likely to explore the CRM system and look for proactive ways to squeeze out every possible bit of value.

Extended Use and the Design Hierarchy of Needs

The CRM adoption challenge faces us daily, and only by ongoing cultivation and user feedback can we allow CRM to evolve and add further organizational value. Extended and postadoptive use can only be realized when the foundational usage which provided the precursor to a user's ability to embark upon extended use is preserved. When ongoing CRM initiatives threaten to compromise the core functionality or technical foundations upon which users have relied, users' ability to engage the CRM at the highest level will be derailed—perhaps not permanently—but for a time.

We can draw an analogy to this notion of what we might call "stacked usage" by reviewing the design hierarchy of needs discussed in an earlier chapter. Recall that the design hierarchy outlines necessary conditions for users to engage the software at each successive level and the levels are arranged as a triangle. The levels are (from the top of the triangle working down) as follows:

- Creativity
- Proficiency
- Usability
- Reliability
- Functionality

Users realistically need a CRM system of quality sufficient to allow them to operate at one of the top two levels of the hierarchy: proficiency or creativity. Keep in mind that some areas of the system may be operating at a lower level, whereas other areas have achieved higher levels. This is more common in environments where CRM is servicing multiple user groups. Ultimately, we are always striving to advance our CRM system up to the highest level of the hierarchy, but here we note specifically the hierarchy's direct impact on influencing users' ability to embrace extended and postadoptive use.

Implementation Partners and Postadoption

When it comes to understanding postadoptive use, it may be prudent to have discussions with consulting partners to understand whether their teams' strengths are best leveraged when part of the core implementation or if extended support and evaluation of functionality usage is a good use of their abilities. Some teams have developed extremely effective implementation skills but may feel out of place in ongoing support. Given the latter is the context through which to observe and promote postadoptive use, the outcome of this discussion will be highly relevant to developing an ongoing approach. An interview with a leading CRM consultant highlighted the difference in various consultants' orientation. When asked about his observations on postadoptive use, he noted,

> My personal preference is not to stay too long after the implementation because our implementation team isn't playing to its strengths. We're focused on the build and the better we can leverage that strength, the better off everyone is. I would prefer that post-implementation, a transition to the support team, is a clean and quick hand-off. They're the ones who need to be most familiar with an implementation over time. The drawback to a quick hand-off is you do lose that insight to say "Were we successful here? How can we measure this to understand if we've achieved our goals?" There are tradeoffs. Generally I think a 3 month post go-live support model makes sense—ramping down the implementation team and handing-off to the support team.[3]

These sentiments speak to the importance of keeping internal support teams deeply involved throughout the implementation itself. Once they have achieved a sufficient level of knowledge of the system's features, they will be better positioned to identify, quantify, and evangelize postadoptive use. The CRM governance team can assist in these success measurements first by prioritizing the capture of user behaviors and next by devoting resources to the analysis of such behaviors. An organization should be very clear as to exactly what metrics it values in the postadoptive stage. While extended, postadoptive, use is a good predictor of adoption, consider an organization with 1000 users and 10 have embraced postadoptive use. It would be difficult to make the case that the system has been well adopted unless basic adoption can be proven for a large population of the remaining users.

We have focused on technology quality throughout this book, highlighting it as a necessary precursor to adoption. According to a 2011 study, if we do have poor technology quality and somehow, through sheer force of will, by mandating usage or other means, we are able to drag some users into a postadoptive mindset and keep those users engaged, this engagement will facilitate extended use by "mitigating the negative effects of low technology quality."[1] We were unable to find other studies supporting this sentiment, but it may be encouraging to firms that have struggled with poor technical implementations.

In other words, keeping folks bought-in throughout the process may actually ease concerns about bad technology. Ideally, the combination of user involvement with guidance from CRM experts should have resulted in a technologically strong CRM. Even if it did not, however, this study shows us exactly how powerful user involvement is. Having now synthesized a large body of adoption literature along with expert sentiments from the field, we cannot understate the criticality of user involvement given that it can drive adoption even in circumstances where the odds are stacked against it. We maintain, however, that technology quality is imperative to all CRM success, including achieving postadoptive use.

Chapter Summary

In this chapter, we have examined the concepts of extended and postadoptive CRM use. While we understand that a focus on core functionality (recall our 80/20 rule—20% of functionality can bring 80% of the benefit) is critical, a properly engineered CRM system can facilitate extended or postadoptive use. We have seen that such usage has the potential to bring significant benefit from CRM. Firms seeking validation of the relative success of their CRM initiatives should include an assessment of level of usage. Recall that extent of usage was one of the factors missing from the TAM, but has been the subject of additional research. We have seen that postadoptive use can only take place when processes and software are performing at one of the two highest levels of the design hierarchy of needs: proficiency or, ideally, creativity.

We have examined the role of outside implementation partners in the context of extended use: namely that such resources have both the preference and expertise to focus on the implementation but may prefer to transition ongoing support and training to internal resources. The underlying paradigm is that various resources perform best in certain contexts. We would hope, however, that external implementation partners will choose (budget permitting) to hang around a bit longer postimplementation so that they can acquire knowledge of the unique challenges faced during this portion of the CRM life cycle and use these insights to make decisions throughout future implementations. In addition to robust processes and technology, pursuing strong support structures, embracing ongoing training, and enlisting evangelists will be effective in promoting extended and postadoptive use. We will discuss evangelism further in the next chapter.

References

1. Hsieh, J. P.-A., Rai, A., & Xu, S. X. (2011). Extracting business value from IT: A sensemaking perspective of post-adoptive use. *Management Science 57(11)*, 2018–2039.
2. Clark, P., Rocco, R. A., & Bush, A. J. (2007). Sales force automation systems and sales force productivity: Critical issues and research agenda. *Journal of Relationship Marketing 6(2)*, 67–87.
3. Anonymous. (2016, January 12–13). Making CRM successful—CRM practitioner interview (S. J. Kinnett, Interviewer).

18

ONGOING AND FUTURE INITIATIVES

We understand that customer relationship management (CRM) is not a point in time phenomenon but rather a holistic strategy supported by a technological foundation. Much focus has been placed on the implementation of CRM given its criticality in setting the stage for a firm's CRM success. Over time, we will invariably find ourselves looking to grow CRM. Ideally, by the time we are ready to expand CRM, we will have already achieved extended use of the initially deployed functionality or at least gotten solid usage on basic functions. We know from the design hierarchy of needs, revisited in the prior chapter, that achieving the pinnacle level of creativity may cause users to develop a zealousness for those functions they hold dear. Imagine now, if a new CRM initiative threatened those functions.

Even in the best of circumstances, we have had to be on guard against resentment and cynicism, but in the face of threatening users' ability to use the system to the extent they wish, such resentment and cynicism will be magnified 10-fold. This echoes a sentiment by one of the practitioners interviewed for this book, who noted many organizations want to jump right into CRM—including ongoing initiatives surrounding CRM—without being strategic about these decisions. If a future initiative compromises the existing abilities for users to interact with the system creatively and make the most of the insights it provides, users will be frustrated by what they will perceive as inconsistent management cues. From a user's perspective, "They say they want me to get the most out of the system, but then they ruin it." We are now quite familiar with the importance of top management support and the importance of top management communicating clear and unambiguous positions. Ensuring consistent management messaging and achieving buy-in from existing system users are paramount.

If organizations disregard recommendations such as facilitating a simple design or take shortcuts with integration or fail to provide adequate ongoing user education, it initially may seem that these missteps have not yielded the catastrophic consequences we have outlined. In some cases, these mistakes might not cause pain immediately. Sometimes organizations are able to drag even the most bloated implementations across the finish line. Over time, however, they will begin to see incremental challenges. One of our consultants noted in our discussion of system customization the challenge of bringing in engineers to work on the system going forward, noting that over-customization will require them to dissect others' code, leading to increased costs and risks. In general, resourcing requirements will grow.

In prior chapters, we have touched upon the importance of guarding against too many changes in CRM (such as the "add another checkbox" trap). We realize that CRM systems will need to accommodate changes over time. Our goal is to allow our CRM to age gracefully. A well-functioning governance structure will be integral to this process, as well as strong evangelism persisting beyond initial rollout. Cross-functional collaboration—integral for any type of organizational success—can be improved by pursuing employee alignment exercises. Firms can consider to some degree ongoing system changes as analogous to their core CRM implementation. We strive for simplicity, we gain stakeholder and user consensus, we preserve the technical integrity of the CRM system, we train thoroughly, and we devote resources to ongoing evangelism.

Evangelism

Evangelism is a key component of achieving CRM success and it could have appeared in many sections of this book. When we think about evangelism—promoting the software and process—we see parallels to the concept of technology positioning we first explored in Chapter 6. Recall that positioning the Technology Division involves changing the way that employees view the division along a continuum of competency, credibility, and commitment. A significant portion of this process occurs in the context of senior management and outside of daily system users. Evangelism is an opportunity not only to increase awareness of and excitement around CRM features but also to improve the way users of CRM view the Technology Division more broadly.

For all its promises, evangelism does carry some level of risk. We know that creating system champions and evangelists comes with risk of resentment and cynicism by colleagues when the CRM fails to deliver on core expectations. Evangelists have little hope of succeeding with a grossly inferior product. A product with limitations can be evangelized by focusing on what the system does well and previewing future improvements to address those pain points raised by users. The more evangelists can frame the system in terms of how easy it is to use, the better the odds of success. We explored within the training chapter the importance of trainers reinforcing the idea that the system is easy to use. Naturally, just like trainers, evangelists must be so adept at using the system that they can position the system as being easy to use. These recommendations are direct results of our core adoption foundations explored in our discussion of the technology acceptance model (TAM) and its descendants.

Evangelism at times seems to be a role merged with either a trainer or perhaps a business analyst. Naturally the efficacy of this model is predicated on the importance placed upon and, as a corollary, the percentage of time allocated to the evangelist function. With all the demands of project work and the natural tendency to become comfortable with a deployed system that basically works and has a reasonable level of adoption, it is easy to see the evangelist function becoming a smaller and smaller component of an employee's time.

As with support resources, evangelists are natural champions of the users and will, through their daily activities, gain insights difficult to obtain through other means, especially if the issue did not result in engagement with the support team (e.g., no application error occurred). Creating a feedback loop where evangelists have a direct line to the CRM governance team and are able to raise users' concerns quickly and effectively will allow rapid development of initiatives to address these concerns. Even in organizations where evangelists are defined as a singular role, distinct from, for example, the training function, they remain the natural partners of trainers and CRM knowledge managers.

Evangelism could be viewed as nice to have within an organization. Indeed a quick search on any career board for evangelist positions of this nature will yield few results. While we are not suggesting any IT role does not carry importance, we have evidence to show that the evangelist function might have particular benefits for CRM. If organizations are truly serious about yielding the maximum benefits from their CRM initiatives, it is difficult to envision a scenario where some level of evangelism would not be necessary to ensure ongoing interest and cultivate extended use from the CRM system. One point we have noted earlier during our discussion of the design hierarchy of needs is that if a system achieves the level of proficiency or, even better, creativity, users then have the potential to become natural evangelists as they gain value from their continued use of the system.

CRM Transformation

We understand that CRM can have myriad users, though we have focused almost exclusively on CRM's (and its predecessor, sales force automation's) original user base: salespeople. As we implement CRM, we may have initially implemented the system for salespeople and, as an example, client service representatives. Given the current ecosystem of packaged software, and as we saw in our chapter exploring CRM integrations, CRM is rapidly expanding out of its original functionality to, in many cases, evolve into an enterprise resource planning (ERP) system serving multiple user groups across various functional areas in the organization.

One risk that occurs with the expansion of CRM to be not just a tool to automate sales and marketing and often system support is the familiar but heightened risk of over-architecture and decreased performance. Many packaged products provide opportunities to configure custom presentation per user group—or even multiple screen layouts intragroup—and we recommend these be fully embraced. As we implement new features for additional user groups, remaining vigilant and continually asking the question: "How will this impact our existing users?" will remain paramount to ongoing CRM success. Diverting resources to implement CRM for existing user groups may also decrease responsiveness to sales concerns and requests for new features, so expectation management will play an integral part in retaining all of the hard-earned gains we realized during initial implementation.

Expansion of CRM utilization should go hand in hand with expansion of all manner of technology resources including support personnel, trainers, and evangelists in addition to engineers. It can be tempting to believe that since the core platform remains the same that existing resources can absorb the additional user groups but such a posture risks CRM failure. Additionally, expanding the CRM landscape to additional user groups in implementing functionality to handle more than fundamental CRM operations will necessitate an expanded governance structure. In addition to all of the actors we discussed in our chapter about governance, we now have the responsibility to add stakeholders and users from the new business units. Does this risk falling into the trap of having too many cooks in the kitchen? Absolutely. But an incomplete governance model creates far too fertile a breeding ground for users to feel ignored and their opinions unvalued—conditions which could hardly be riper to induce user resistance.

Overall, we can see that expanding CRM to accommodate business units traditionally served by other systems and processes comes with the benefits of a single data repository, the ability potentially to retire legacy systems, and consolidate Technology resources. At the same time, expanding CRM introduces a number of risks including compromising core functionality and performance, reducing an organization's ability to accommodate requests, and increasing the time required for stakeholders and users to gain consensus on the future of the system. While expanding CRM to be a full-service enterprise platform may well be the future, we must ensure we do not compromise core CRM fundamentals.

Chapter Summary

In this chapter, we have reviewed the state of CRM post rollout and the landscape most conducive to ongoing CRM success. Namely, as originally noted in our chapter discussing training, we want to continue to demonstrate to users that CRM is an evolving product, which will add value not only as a point in time solution but on an ongoing basis with new features being released periodically. We want to continue to remember that we can benefit from viewing features through a broad lens—not just new buttons to click. Improving system response time is a feature—perhaps resulting from a review of configuration decisions and revising such choices to yield a more elegant and responsive structure.

We have explored the importance of evangelism and continuing education to ensure CRM remains top of mind and is perceived as a system continually growing to add greater and greater value to the business without compromising core principles. We examined the importance of scaling not just the system but also corresponding support resources and the CRM governance structure. The evolution of CRM to perform more and more functions is a reality already embraced by many organizations, but it requires the same amount of diligence, if not more, than our initial implementation.

Finally, we have examined the implications of expanding CRM's remit to serve as a tool beyond simply managing relationships, but also for various back-office functions such as billing, or even as a full-scale ERP solution. We now see that in order to succeed with the transformation of CRM, we must focus upon securing buy-in from additional stakeholders while increasing resourcing and support to ensure the additional user base does not have an inferior experience. At the same time, we must ensure that core users' needs do not get lost and too much attention is paid to the "new guys." Along with the need for expanded governance and representation, we have seen that pursuing system expansion includes the mandate to not compromise existing functionality.

19

Making CRM Successful

We now arrive at the end of our hero's journey to achieve customer relationship management (CRM) success. We have been down a long road. We have explored a vast landscape of factors that must be mastered to achieve the value we want from CRM. The reality that we have spent hundreds of pages exploring considerations necessary for success tells us volumes in itself about the challenges facing CRM practitioners. Given the rapid expansion in organizational expenditures on CRM initiatives, it is clear that firms are eager to realize all the purported benefits of CRM, but the daunting rates of failure and the quantity of projects that are reimplementations of CRM underscore the importance of firms reviewing the insights we have explored throughout this text.

We began by presenting what many consider to be a contrarian view of what is necessary for CRM success. That is, specific technology choices are instrumental in influencing an organization's potential of achieving CRM success. While the technology—in the sense of having a product that can be configured and customized extensively—might not be a core problem, the implementation of poor, convoluted business processes into the technology is what results in a poor technological environment. We would posit that jamming poor business processes into a CRM system would pervert even the most robust packaged software solution, underscoring the reality that technology cannot correct poor processes.

So, those who advise a focus on process over technology are correct, in the sense that process must be in good working order when analyzed outside the context of the particular technology implementation. As it relates to the specific technology, it is certainly true that both good and bad business processes could result in a poor technology outcome. The former—strong business processes but poor technology outcomes—are likely due to implementation deficiencies. Having good processes is no guarantee that the implementation will result in a robust and sustainable technology landscape, but it is certainly a move in the right direction.

We have discussed that measuring CRM success can, in itself, be a nebulous undertaking, and such success can be evaluated through a number of measurements beyond a firm's revenue such as operational efficiency. Quantifying CRM success, however, is less important than focusing on the process that would yield such success. A process over outcome mentality allows firms to remain focused on adoption and evangelism. Some firms may find themselves looking for success metrics (the outcome) when time would be better spent ensuring they focus on ensuring the CRM runs efficiently, is free of defects, and is seeing extended, postadoptive use from the user base.

We have examined how CRM can be categorized as strategic, operational, analytical, or social. In this book, we have primarily examined strategic and operational CRM as mastery of these two facets of the overall CRM landscape provides the best hope for long-term success. We have examined the importance of mastering operational fundamentals before attempting to dive into more extensive functionality such as data analytics. It is not necessarily the complexity of implementing the actual analytics engine that is concerning, but rather how these initiatives often lead to perversion of the CRM system by increasing the number of data points required to perform basic operational tasks, even if these data points have not been shown to yield insights.

Knowing Your Audience

We have seen that CRM has rapidly expanded from its infancy as a sales force automation (SFA) tool to an enterprise platform which is in some cases the hub from which organizations run their businesses. In this text, we have primarily focused on salespeople both because they remain the core user base of CRM and because research and experience have shown that they can be among the most difficult users to satisfy. We have learned that salesperson resistance is rampant for a number of reasons, including perceived role conflict when salespeople find themselves diverting time from selling in order to deal with CRM systems. Evidence has further shown that, for whatever underlying reasons, salespeople have demonstrated themselves to be the most change-resistant and fearful of technology of all white-collar workers. Understanding these realities both establishes the challenges of CRM as distinct from enterprise systems aligned to other audiences and also provides insights into strategies to manage the user base.

Revisiting Organizational Readiness and Culture

Recall one sentiment from our chapter discussing organizational readiness which bluntly informed us that a functioning company with good financial results does not imply that the company runs efficiently or has properly defined its objectives and responsibilities. The theme of achieving mastery of fundamentals before delving into more advanced initiatives also applies to an organization even outside the context of CRM. It is important to remember that CRM is only a component of broader sales, marketing, and technology climates. To the latter, about a dozen barriers to entry have been identified that we recommend firms remedy before embarking on CRM initiatives, including weakness in customer strategy, immaturity of the organization's technology and information systems, poor internal communication, goal ambiguity, deficiencies in project management, and inter-functional conflict.

One of the most applicable barriers to entry is the presence of deficiencies in existing technical systems or processes. For firms finding themselves with challenges within their core operational landscape, such as poor phones or insufficient hardware, they will enter CRM initiatives with a disadvantage. Employees operating with core inefficiencies or other factors that degrade professional quality of life (such as working with a single monitor when two are needed to function effectively, achieve flow, and decrease multitasking) will enter all initiatives at a disadvantage, suggesting, once again, that effective execution of fundamentals starting with core infrastructure remains paramount to our success.

In the classic self-improvement book *The Magic of Thinking Big*, David J. Schwarz devotes a chapter to the importance of managing one's environment. Specifically, he notes that creating a first-class environment has direct consequences on all aspects of one's life. Examples of such an environment are wearing nice clothes, reducing clutter on desks and around the house or office, and surrounding ourselves with high-quality people. If operational conditions have already created—outside of the particulars of CRM—an environment that breeds resistance, how can we expect that resistance not to bleed into CRM? We would enter the CRM landscape with a handicap, and, as we have seen, succeeding with CRM is difficult enough without preexisting issues.

Understanding Adoption

While firms seek many benefits from their CRM initiatives, literature and experience have shown that these benefits are all but impossible to achieve without successful adoption of the CRM system by its users. As a result, we have explored a number of theoretical underpinnings to enable us to pursue adoption intelligently. The core model that can drive many of our CRM decisions is the technology acceptance model (TAM), a construct which states that users' perceptions of how easy the technology is to use (perceived ease of use) influences perceptions of how useful the technology is (perceived usefulness), which in turn influences users to adopt the software. The model suggests that users are unlikely to perceive a system as useful if it is not easy to use. We understand, however, that a system could exist which is easy to use but fails to deliver key functionality. In such a scenario, users would perceive the system as easy to use and as such that the system is useful, even though the system is not actually useful. But adoption is largely predicated on user perception, and as such, we are unlikely to persuade users that the software is useful if it is not easy to use, even if—objectively—the software is highly useful.

We understand that critiques of the TAM posit that it is too simplistic and fails to take into account a number of other variables that could influence adoption. This critique is justified and led to future research and the unified theory of the acceptance and use of technology (UTAUT). This model supplemented the TAM with the theory of rational action (TRA), the motivational model, the theory of planned behavior (TPB) model of PC utilization, innovation diffusion theory, and social cognitive theory. The resulting UTAUT encompasses four major dimensions: performance expectancy, effort expectancy, social expectancy, and facilitating expectancy. We have explored primarily the social expectancy variables—e.g., peer pressure and subjective norm—as factors observed as significant in both professional contexts and throughout academic research and which can directly inform our approaches to gamification along with incentive and training programs. A deeper examination of the other variables encompassing the UTAUT on CRM is a prime topic for future texts.

Alignment

Achieving alignment between business units and the Technology Division is of paramount importance for firms to achieve success not only with CRM but also with other enterprise technology initiatives. We now understand that alignment is the successful achievement of harmony between business processes and the technology supporting these processes. One alignment definition we explored captured a facet of alignment which is at times missing: the circular relationship between business units and the technology which supports them. Remember that the business influences the technology; the technology influences the business.

We now understand that alignment not only extends beyond the harmony of processes and the technical implementation of technology to execute these processes, but it also occurs in the context through which different employees within an organization interact with one another. Recall the concept of employee alignment. When employees are aligned, they are joined by common language, trust, and knowledge. Without pursuing opportunities for cross-functional collaboration and knowledge sharing, employees are left with a mutual ignorance of their colleagues' contributions to the organization and the challenges their colleagues face. In the context of a CRM implementation, poor employee alignment can result in incomplete or misunderstood requirements elicitation, longer implementation times, and negative—if unjustified—perceptions of the Technology Division. Alignment can be improved by fostering trust, increasing cross-functional collaboration, and implementing a common vocabulary across business units and the Technology Division.

Positioning the Technology Division

We have examined the importance of the relationship between business units and the Technology Division, and how the Technology Division can work to position itself as a trusted business partner. Succeeding with this challenge begins by assessing where the division stands within the technology maturity model. This model posits that the division will be viewed as performing at one of three levels: competency, credibility, or commitment. The division can benefit first by pursuing initiatives to demonstrate competency via robust, durable systems and superior support. Once these goals have been achieved, the Technology Division can seek to demonstrate its credibility by delivering projects on time, within budget, and through effectively satisfying business objectives. Finally, the division will achieve commitment, a state in which business units view the division as a trusted, strategic partner whose insights play a critical role in the organization's decision-making and ongoing strategy.

The Technology Division can benefit by embracing a marketing lens, a posture where it views structures, processes, and relationships as if they were contributing to the delivery of a product. This posture fits well with the paradigm we discussed called promotion orientation. Too often, Technology has to play defense, assume the standard cost-center posture, and minimize the potential for failure instead of being empowered to strive and promote itself as a driver of innovation. We know that so many cultural, contextual, and process factors contribute to CRM success, but make no mistake: the sophistication of the Technology Division and its ability to progress to the top level of maturity will play indispensable roles in achieving CRM success.

Governance

We learned in our discussion of governance that the historical foundations through which governance models were developed were notably deficient in the technical component. As organizations sought to remedy this deficiency, they began to focus primarily on data governance. While this focus was beneficial and a step in the right direction, we now understand that governance extends beyond data and is just as, if not more, important when it comes to the implementation of new functionality and the evolution or removal of existing functionality. We recall that governance structures are at times most effective when they look for ways to make CRM simpler and less reactive to knee-jerk organizational initiatives.

We now understand that governance structures such as the steering committee benefit from robust involvement from many areas of the organization including the user base, senior management, the Technology Division, and support personnel, regardless of where they sit within the organization. As a result of the need for such representation, we risk analysis paralysis and having too many cooks in the kitchen. This reality can be mitigated by ensuring that the voices of those participants who are less senior in the organizational hierarchy—such as support personnel or those users chosen to represent their business units—are given equal voice as senior personnel who are likely more disconnected from the day-to-day realities of CRM.

The Partner–Vendor Paradigm

We explored the importance of the posture an organization takes toward its external implementation providers along with any contractors they bring on internally. Evidence has shown that treating these individuals as partners and not just vendors or contactors is a critical component of achieving CRM success. Indeed, implementation providers themselves are also influenced by this effective positioning exercise. When they are treated as trusted partners, they will naturally find themselves working even harder to deliver a quality result, whether they realize they are trying harder or not.

The Importance of Business Analysis

We have explored the importance of the business analysis function, arriving at an understanding that—while all aspects of the project life cycle are important—some of the greatest challenges and unanticipated project costs are a results of deficiencies in business analysis. Requirements elicitation is often incomplete, and missed requirements present a number of unique challenges as teams scramble to plug holes often in less elegant ways than they would have addressed the issues had they been included in the initial scope.

Next, we examined ways to ensure the business analysis function can succeed. For example, we now know that dividing a business analyst's time across myriad functions beyond business analysis, such as project management or technical design, not only decreases the quality of the business analysis component, but it may also cause firms to make ill-advised hiring decisions.

Finally, we examined several techniques which firms can employ during the business analysis process to aid them in achieving a quality outcome. Some of the most important of these techniques surround requirements capture and management. Eliciting requirements through multiple modes has shown itself to be effective. User shadowing, in particular, can provide opportunities to identify functions users may not even have been aware they were performing. Group interviews may uncover a broader perspective on requirements and provide a forum to resolve potential disagreements. At the same time, some users may not feel empowered, perhaps as a result of a fear of embarrassment, to speak up. This diminishes the effectiveness of the workshop setting, which necessitates the need for individual interviews, which can often be built into the shadowing process.

To Customize or Not to Customize

The decision to purchase packaged software comes with the implicit assumption that the system can be crafted to satisfy the unique needs of each organization. We now understand that this is a half-truth. While some will say that CRM can do anything and everything, what we are left with from the extant literature and professionals' observations is that CRM success relies so heavily on user buy-in of the system that twisting the system to meet that one extra "very important" business requirement could jeopardize adoption if the requirement compromises user experience. As CRM continues to widen in its scope to become not just an SFA tool with some marketing features to a full enterprise platform upon which many organizations run the bulk of their businesses, our advice and that of the extant research may begin to seem more and more antiquated.

After all, the business wants to take CRM to its limits, push the envelope, and make it all things to all people. As practitioners with varying levels of influence, we may find ourselves without many options (aside from asking stakeholders to read this book to gain an understanding of the implications of their requests), but even if we find ourselves forced to mutate CRM in a direction which does not align with our own recommendations, we remain empowered to focus on areas we might still have the power to influence, such as user education, strong governance, consistent alignment initiatives, and gamification. We may not win every customization battle, but we can educate others on the implications of their requests and perhaps succeed in securing extra resources to help support the expanding remit placed upon our CRM system.

User Involvement

We have discussed the importance of user involvement throughout the implementation process and beyond. In particular, we realize that we want to involve users, but we must guard against allowing them to pull us away from our own instincts and expertise as practitioners. To our users who are reading, we ask you to understand that your opinions are valuable—indeed we have gone to extremes to ensure user needs are met—but our concern is that when users are taken completely at face value, they can steamroll through the recommendations of consultants and experts. Since the importance of involving users has become more and more apparent in recent years, it is natural to allow the pendulum to swing too far in the direction as taking their opinions as sacrosanct. Sometimes, we must protect users from themselves, and it is our responsibility to take strong positions when we believe their approaches are misguided.

We have also learned that people in general are predisposed to spend the majority of time discussing the least important matters. This commonly manifests during discussions of how fields should be arranged on screens within the system. Users—and to be fair, some practitioners—will tend to spend inordinate amounts of time on such decisions because they feel their opinions are more relevant and they are more comfortable speaking on that topic compared to, for example, complicated process improvements.

User Education

During our discussion of user training and education, we learned that these initiatives are not point-in-time efforts but rather ongoing initiatives to be integrated into organizational culture. We now understand that some organizations may provide strong onboarding training but fall short of integrating robust CRM training into that process. Treating CRM as part of core curriculum in the same way as, say, filling out time sheets, will position CRM in a more prominent position within employees' minds. We have also seen evidence of the importance of including core technical literacy in the onboarding training curriculum.

We have learned about the importance of management making its cues around training clear and unambiguous, including their position toward how they position training as a mandatory initiative. Management decisions will be perceived differently by users of varying demographics. Similarly, we have learned that educational approaches should be tailored to an audience. More mature and experienced salespeople, for example, tend to be less inclined to participate or even attend large group sessions, sometimes feeling that they will be judged by others if they ask remedial questions which are already evident to others.

The mentor model has been shown to be effective with more experienced salespeople. They can be paired with a more technically savvy member of the user base and learn in a more one-on-one setting. One challenge with the mentor model is it is difficult to track the extent to which training is occurring and any mistakes which the mentor might make in his instruction would be hard to identify. This could lead mentees to develop poor habits. Ultimately, as with trainer selection, we need to ensure that mentors are highly competent in their skills. We have also learned that we should create a portfolio of training methods including tactical video modules, formal classroom training sessions, mentoring, cheat sheets, and ongoing "Did you know?" recommendations for efficient and effective system usage.

Big Data

The promises of superior customer insights resulting from effective data analytics have sent many firms flocking toward big data initiatives. As they attempt to capture more and more pieces of customer data to populate their data warehouses and feed their analytics engines, firms must guard against inadvertently compromising user adoption. The danger is attempting to cram more and more fields into CRM screens, with the ambiguous hope that these data will later become useful. Instead, firms will benefit from defining exactly what insights they wish to achieve and let those definitions drive decisions on data capture. In order to realize gains from analytical CRM, firms must first master operational CRM.

We have explored external data stewards and providers. While great in concept, some evidence suggests that some of these stewards have ample room to improve. In addition, a great deal of planning will be necessary for the successful integration of an external data steward. To succeed with external data stewardship initiatives, firms should set guidelines around communication, define field-level ownership, and set expectations surrounding stewards' responsibilities and expected frequency of updates.

Support

We have seen evidence that some organizations are beginning to understand the value of the support function. Career opportunities within the support function have at times been lacking, particularly when the role is viewed as a precursor to other opportunities such as business analysis. As the support function continues to evolve to a level where support representatives are able to deliver complete solutions on the spot, firms will benefit from creating opportunities for advancement. Support representatives, given their close proximity to the user base, are valuable contributors to both governance structures and to the business analysis function during future projects.

In addition to strategic placement of the support function, we have examined particulars surrounding the implementation of support, including in the context of support ticket construction. Firms can benefit by reducing complexities in the support process, which may be as straightforward as removing fields that are not truly useful in resolving support cases. Just as we risk compromising successful implementation of operational CRM by cramming in data points in hopes that they will be beneficial to a future analytics engine, we should be real with ourselves about exactly what actions will be taken based on the capture of various data points within support tickets.

Extended Use

We have seen that most of CRM's core value is realized through execution of daily fundamentals. If we have created a quality system, however, users may be empowered to embrace extended or post-adoptive functionality: features which are not imperative to daily operations but have the potential to extract notable value from the CRM system. We understand that the ability of users to embrace such usage is directly predicated on our ability to provide technology which achieves one of the top two levels of the design hierarchy of needs. Those levels, proficiency and creativity, provide a technology climate conducive to exploration. It is the mastery of the first three levels that—not unlike the relationships in Maslow's hierarchy of needs—provides the space, the feeling of safety, to embark on further adventures within the system.

We discussed in Chapter 14 on user education that the main curriculum particularly in the classroom should focus exclusively on core functionality. Extended use is largely taken on by users without guidance, though technical evangelists have an important role to play as they partner with trainers to ensure those users who are ready to realize additional value from CRM have the knowledge to do so. Adjunct support resources like video tutorials are a good way to introduce users to extended features without overwhelming them.

Ongoing Initiatives

We understand that CRM is not a point-in-time initiative but an ongoing process. We want to view CRM as a product that continually evolves. As we have seen, CRM has—for many firms—been expanded to be so much more than a tool to manage customer relationship and automated sales force tasks. CRM is now the hub from which many organizations run their most vital business functions. As organizations continue to look for ways to expand CRM, we want to remain true to our core mission of adhering to fundamentals, simplifying wherever we can and ensuring that when CRM is expanded, that new business units receive proper training, guidance, and support.

Firms can benefit by reviewing their system periodically to identify opportunities to remove extraneous fields that may no longer be relevant. Think of it as spring cleaning. Anything, no matter how miniscule, that might impact our users' ability to embrace CRM and integrate it effectively into their work processes should be removed. Not only does this exercise provide benefits for users, but it also reminds stakeholders and practitioners of past decisions and hopefully provides insights to drive more effective future decisions.

If Things Do Not Go as Planned

Even armed with all of these insights, we remain humble, understanding that succeeding with CRM is remarkably challenging. If it were easy, everyone would have achieved success. This book—and all the other books and articles written about CRM—would not be necessary. If it were easy, we would not see so many CRM projects occur in the reimplementation space. To that end, do not fear or be discouraged if you find the need to embark on a reimplementation of your CRM program—be it from cultural, functional, or technical perspectives.

Do not be intimidated by seemingly endless lists of organizational preconditions that have been shown to be required to have a shot at CRM success. Sometimes, the sales function will attempt to rush CRM implementations, but far better first to assess the organization and see if any areas are deficient—particularly the top areas most important to CRM as outlined in our discussion of organizational readiness including immaturity of systems or technical processes, weakness of internal communication and cross-functional collaboration, and lack of a customer or change-oriented culture. CRM creates opportunities for organizations to learn about and, often, make changes to its culture and the way it operates, and those opportunities can either be embraced or be ignored to the organization's benefit or peril.

Simply by reading this book, you have taken a huge leap forward in contributing to your organization's potential to be successful with CRM. It would be easy to get discouraged if, even after so much hard work, aspects of CRM do not go as planned. Take a frank assessment of what could have gone wrong, or gone better, without badgering or blaming, and resolve to fix it next time. Begin crafting a business case, as needed, to address the deficiencies you have identified, even if that means scaling back the scope of what you expect CRM to accomplish at this stage of its existence within the organization.

Closing Thoughts

More and more organizations are making financial expenditures to implement CRM. As we noted in Chapter 1, CRM initiatives are rapidly increasing as many firms seek to capitalize on all of CRM's promises. Many will embark on the CRM quest, but few will succeed. Will your firm be one of those elusive success stories? Like many challenges, we wish the answers to the mysteries of CRM success were glamorous or special, shiny and iconoclastic. We want it to be a certain way, but it is not. CRM success is forged in the mastery of fundamentals and disseminating knowledge of those fundamentals in a way that drives adoption and increases users' ability to succeed, be it in sales, marketing, support, or otherwise. Understanding the elegance that comes with simplicity, we must not allow ourselves to be seduced by the ease of configuring and customizing packaged software solutions. In one respect, we can see that achieving CRM success is borne of restraint. Stakeholders may not intuitively grasp this paradigm, and that failure to accept certain operational realities plays a significant role in the frustration borne from CRM failures.

Let us be sure that we set realistic expectations with our stakeholders about exactly what we hope to gain and what is reasonable to gain from CRM. Given the hyperbole that permeates CRM vendors' marketing materials and sales pitches, it is far too easy to expect CRM to do everything but pick up our dry cleaning. Practitioners who follow the guidance we have explored may achieve strong operational gains—which we now know are the foundation to further success—but not see an immediate change in revenue. If stakeholders go into a project expecting CRM outcomes to result in the organization's meteoric rise to the top of their industry, anything less unfairly paints practitioners, project team members, and the Technology Division. Some of the gains resulting from successful CRM may be intangible, and others may take years to fully realize.

CRM salvation is within reach. Focus on fundamentals, listen to users, procure the advice of experts, and remember the importance of culture, collaboration, and winning the hearts and minds. And don't forget about the technology. You—and your organization—have to believe that CRM really *matters*. It is not an ancillary initiative, not a nice-to-have, not the subject of mere lip service from top management. It is the posture of the organization, the commitment to mastering the purest of business functions: cultivating superior customer relationships. As CRM goes, so goes the firm.

Index